SWORD DANCE

SWORD DANCE

A WOMAN'S STORY
A CELTIC POEM

VERONICA GAYLIE

EXILE
editions

Library and Archives Canada Cataloguing in Publication

Gaylie, Veronica, author
Sword dance : a woman's story -- a Celtic poem / VeronicaGaylie.

Issued in print and electronic formats.
ISBN 978-1-55096-433-2 (pbk.).--ISBN 978-1-55096-434-9 (pdf).--
ISBN 978-1-55096-480-6 (epub).--ISBN 978-1-55096-481-3 (mobi)

I. Title.

PS8613.A9823S96 2015   C811'.6   C2015-900877-8
                                           C2015-900878-6

Design and Composition by Mishi Uroboros
Typeset in Fairfield font at Moons of Jupiter Studios

Published by Exile Editions Ltd ~ www.ExileEditions.com
144483 Southgate Road 14-GD, Holstein, Ontario, N0G 2A0
Printed and Bound in Canada in 2015, by Marquis Books

We gratefully acknowledge, for their support toward our publishing activities,
the Canada Council for the Arts, the Government of Canada through
the Canada Book Fund, the Ontario Arts Council,
and the Ontario Media Development Corporation.

Conseil des Arts du Canada Canada Council for the Arts Canada

ONTARIO ARTS COUNCIL
CONSEIL DES ARTS DE L'ONTARIO
an Ontario government agency
un organisme du gouvernement de l'Ontario

Ontario
Ontario Media Development Corporation

Canadian Sales: The Canadian Manda Group, 664 Annette Street,
Toronto ON M6S 2C8 www.mandagroup.com 416 516 0911

North American and International Distribution, and U.S. Sales:
Independent Publishers Group, 814 North Franklin Street,
Chicago IL 60610 www.ipgbook.com toll free: 1 800 888 4741

For my mother
Grace Gallacher Gaylie
of Glasgow

INTRODUCTION

When my mother said the words *scrambled eggs* – you could see them. Homemade. Yellow and fluffy. On a plate. In my mother's Glaswegian accent, every "r" brought waves of salute in honour of the hen who laid them: *scrrram-bellld aaayygs*. The depths of the rrrr's. The pronounced aaa's. You could practically feel the pain the bird went through. You could see before you the fork whisk the egg into something new. Hearing the words in Glaswegian made the transformation from egg to scrambled seem possible, even, poetic. Rather than the deadpan Canadian Scrambled Eggs, hearing the words the Glasgow-way, made you think. Made you sit up and take notice. It made you wonder if there was a bit more to it. Something good. Or something amiss. Something worthy of notice. Saying *scrambled eggs* the Glaswegian way, honours the egg. It seems the very least a human who consumes them, can do.

The Glasgow accent, dialect and language, is a voice of variations and difference. It brings life to life. It brings excitement. Vivid images. Discernment. Decisions. Reverence. Wisdom.

For the magic to happen, the reader/listener of Glaswegian needs to listen for the shifts. The jokes, the lessons, and the wisdom are typically implied. The meaning comes built-in. As you read this book, if you note a shift in tone or a word that is spelled differently from the page before, there is probably something Glaswegian going on. If you turn your head, you might miss it. But then, if you look too hard, the variations might perplex. The Glaswegian does not give up her meaning easily, or in the usual way. If the narrator's voice switches from the mother to the daughter to the aunt to the uncle, then that character is taking over the story and kicking the ball a little ways further down the field. The names of the narrator's grandparents (her grandparents) are usually "the mither/the faither" no matter whose talking. Sometimes the punch-line lands on a line below. This is communal storytelling. Sometimes, you just run with it.

The origins of the Glasgow patter, or Glaswegian vernacular, are rooted in the grit and grime of the sooty city. During the 19th and 20th centuries, many moved from Ireland and the Scottish Highlands to Glasgow for work in factories and nearby mines. The words and inflections rose up and evolved straight from the grind and chatter of the workaday world, among those who likely did not want to leave their birthplace. The source of the language was born from the frustrations, and the fearlessness, of real life.

Glaswegian invites camaraderie. A Glaswegian might leave you with the words: *Take care ay yehs*. The plural is implied. When *yeh* (you) becomes *yehs*, you know you are not alone. As you depart, you can take heart that the Glaswegian team is behind you now with linked arms, ready to defend. With just a four-letter word, a Glaswegian conveys friendship and solidarity. It's like a secret signal, a little gift. To yeh. To ye. To yehs.

There's also: *me* and *mine*. A Glaswegian might ask *Where's meh handbag?* to convey: something neutral; yet slightly urgent; with a hint that something might be amiss. On the other hand, *Where's mah handbag?* might convey humility or slight apprehension; perhaps the purse is empty? A Glaswegian in Canada can also switch into the more proper sounding: *Where is my handbag?* which might make the listener leap up and scour the house to help find the handbag.

Some other fun Glaswegian translations that can indicate increased informality, include: *to* (to, teh, te, tae); of (of, ay); do (do, dae); he (he, eh or ehself); was (was, wis, wiz); and you (ye, yeh, yehs). There is also: *nae* and *not*. As in couldnae (could not); shouldnae (should not); wasnae (was not); didnae (did not), etc. To me, the Glaswegian *nae* – conveys presence. As in: This is me. And I am here. I first wasnae/was *not* there. Or, I first couldnae/could *not* do that. And then, found I *was* there. I then found I *could* do that. In Glaswegian, not – brings transformation, and revelation.

Dialect always depends on who is around. A British army officer might bring about a shift. A reunion of friends after a long separation could inspire new language. A daughter telling her mother's story might change voice – as a mother's voice comes to life, through memory.

Glaswegian is, in the end, a way of talking and of finding oneself in a world that isn't always easy or welcoming. Through language, the Glaswegian finds home and creates home. Sharing a word with a stranger on a Glasgow street, on a bus, or in a shop, brings a sense of unity and excitement. Such connection becomes part of the weaving of daily life. It is a way of getting through each day, together. If you read this work aloud you might find yourself basking in the warmth of human differences. You might find bits of wisdom. Like most oral language, the interpretation is up to you.

A Short Glaswegian Guide appears at the end of this book. This limited glossary invites the reader into the lovely, lilting dialect of the Glaswegian. The Scots bard, Robbie Burns, a farmer's son, was also asked by his publisher to include a glossary in his first book of poetry, *Poems, Chiefly in the Scottish Dialect*, published 200 years ago. The educated elite of Edinburgh required a guide to understand Burns' use of Scottish patois, the language of the ordinary people.

In these times of digital technology, arm's length communication, and even more distant wisdom, the voice of the everyday person still rings true. By reading this work the reader has already quietly joined the anonymous, common majority that is always anti-prestige. As I tell my students, the lives of ordinary people, with their problems and contradictions are way more interesting than the lives of celebrities plastered to magazines at the check-out counter.

Like many first generation Canadians, I grew up with stories in my ears. With this book now in your hands, I invite readers into the poems of real life. I invite you to read or even, sing-a-long, loudly, and with feeling. Read them aloud, to yourself, with others, and pass them around. Glaswegian language and story is, above all, human. In these days of dying dialects, the Glasgow voice shines through, as sacred.

Like scrambled eggs.

Poets of the Kitchen Sink

My mother's hands peel potatoes, wind round
and round like fingers on harp strings,
    kitchen sink
    potato skins
    she sings, *Fast the winds blow,*
fast the da dee, la dee dee dee...
We're havin scrambled eggs.

First the yellow word yellow
then scrambled eggs in a pan, sizzling.
Yeh know what happened te St. Lawrence?
Ach. They roasted ehm. They roasted ehm oan ehs back
and then eh said, "Eh. Ahm done – yeh better turn meh over fellas."
Potatoes flung
oil spits oil
fishes round with a slotted spoon.
There was Mary the first, Mary the treen,
Mary the dee dee dee.
This is what you call a slotted spoon.
Slotted, slot-*ted.*
It's so the oil leaks oot.
Aye, oot.
Eggs slide to wan side,
yellow
on yellow. *Runny part runs down the back. See,*
This is a spatula. Spat-ula. It's flat so yeh can get in behind.
First the flat spat-*ula* to chase runny eggs.
Morning has broken, la da dee-dee,
just like the hmm-hmm.
You have te give the carrots a good scrape.
Aye. Garrburratorr.
Water runs,
garburator gurgles.
That's fer veg. Yes, yerrr veg-e-tables.
Eggs flip on spatula backs,
land on plates,
slotted spoon chases chips
heaps in a bowl
drains on paper,
carrots in the corner.
Nine kids, down eggs,
down chips.
Time for the dishes,
back to the sink.

This dance is performed round and over
two Highland broadswords placed crosswise
on the ground at right angles to each other.[1]

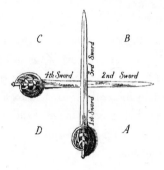

[1] Text: Highland Dancing: The Official Textbook. Scottish Board of Highland Dancing (1955).
Diagrams: Traditional Step Dancing in Scotland. Aberdeen Scottish Cultural Press (1996).

PROLOGUE

Uncle Tom lies in St. Paul's Emergency pacemaker jumping like a sockeye salmon while he teaches two nurses four verses of Danny Boy. They release him and by the time the taxi pulls away eight nurses stand outside waving to him. He says, Cordova Street's the best home he ever had. Three square meals, a radio and people who listen to him sing Hank Williams: lawyers, hockey players, priests and shrinks. My mother says, Ach. He doesnae see the neighbourhood, he jist looks at the flowers.

He spends his days at the courthouse, gets free coffee from the court coffee lady who never in her life gave away anything for free. But Tom has a way about him. He was in fact up to three free coffees a day, overdid it a bit, and the coffee lady had to say, Eh, Tom, I didnae mean it quite like that. Said, I mean, I didnae mean three free coffees noo, and Tom looks up at her and says: You're right, mother. From now oan, it's only wan.

By the time McSorley's hockey trial hit he was back up to three and that day, court packed, standingroom only, the guard said to Tom, Okay, big guy. Go on in. And Tom looked aroond, Big guy? Who's eh talking tae? The way Canadians say things, Tom jist loved it. People in line looked at Tom, who wasnae tall, and said, Hey, why does he get in? And the guard stared back and said, Because he's one of the family.

And Tom went right in.

Later Tom was interviewed on CBC about the trial from an old-timers point of view, except they got Tom who looked straight into the lens with his blue eyes and snowy white hair. Standing there with his free coffee, he said, It was tae hard te see oan TV. Ye really couldnae get a good angle oan things.

The reporter told Tom to walk into the sunset, an oldtimer shot to close the show, *Folks, there goes the oldtimer, walking into the distance, walking slow,* but Tom, camera rolling, live TV, walked slower than they wanted him to. Behind him the camera rolled, the reporter's voice slowed and slowed, tried to keep pace with Tom walking slow: Folkss…there goes the oldtimer…walking…walllkingg…

But Tom walked slower than slow. Tried to drag it out, you know. By the time he pressed the button to cross the street, they liked Tom old, but not so slow.

Now Tom has a way of walking slow. Not like he was before. The night he staggered in circles around the backyard, drunk, shouting,

I'm a fucking Scot!
I'm a fucking Scot!

Before that, he made everyone laugh. Found cigarettes in his ears, made coins disappear. Then, when granda died, he handed in his gloves at the bus mechanic depot and walked and walked and did not stop. All the way to New Westminster.

They gave him electric shock. (I did not care what the neighbours thought.)

Back in Glasgow, he might have been the one with a football kick called The International, but in Canada, he did magic tricks, alone, on the living room loveseat.

I

Although only two swords are used it has been found expedient
to refer to the half blade nearest the dancer's starting place…as the
First Sword, then working in an anti-clockwise direction, referring to
the other half blades as the Second, Third and Fourth Swords.

My mother says in Scotland, every family had a Tom.
Lots had Dicks and Harrys too. It was no joke.
Tom's father was Dick. Dick's father was Tom.
Dick was named after Tom's father, Dick.
Harry was named after Dick's wife's father, Harry.
In Glasgow, no one noticed. Only so many names to go around
and you know how it is over there – everyone shares.

Tom, Dick and Harry wanted to leave Scotland forever.
Everyone nodded. It was understood. Fish and chips only went
so far; life was dull. Souvenirs of Rome over the mantelpiece,
a papal plate, a little ceramic dog that changed colour when it rained;
knick-knacks only went a certain way
til notions of New York called you away.

On the morning the boat left,
waving goodbye to her nephews
the three raw loddies,
Tommy still in boy scout shorts,
the mither saw

> the little blue light on the back of her hand
> that she always saw before bad news.

Over there, the way people leave. You tried and tried
but could not get away. You'd stare at a dripping sink
for years, thinking you had lots of time then, one day,
you'd turn around, see dust falling slowly in the living room sun
and suddenly you'd know a whole life could pass
while that dust fell slow, settling on the shoulders
of a bottle of HP. Then you'd know. (Time to go.)

In the living room after the others left, the other Tom
the mither's son wondered
if he'd ever see North America, the Fraser River, the Pacific Ocean.
He wondered if he'd ever see film star Nelson Eddy as an RCMP
walking out of the Canadian Evergreens.

Thoughts trickled like this in a world of fish and chips
and arguments over where a picture of a soldier should go,
over the mantel or under the bed because a generation before
in Ireland they knew what a picture of a soldier meant.
And up and down from the wall the old picture went:
the father up, the mother down,
no time for it to even leave a mark
of where it might have been.
It was a smoky world.

My mother worked for a chimney sweep in a shack in a lane
because alone, in the coal dust, she could read.

To dream of tap dance shoes, ruby red, in a black and white reel.
To leave a place of chest pains called carbuncles of the heart.
A place of meat pies, neeps, sprouts, cabbage, and the potato.
Later that day
the mither
peeled potatoes for chips, golden,

     how the sun streamed in.

How anyone understood a word
the faither whistled
through his toothless gums:

Where's meh wallies?

He lost the real ones picking up chairs with his teeth to impress the ladies.

Generations stood on the mantelpiece
in photos, in bright hats on vacation,

big smiles
crooked teeth.

Other times it was just the clock in the living room, ticking.
And dust falling. You waited for a sign.
Sure enough someone said,

The day Tom, Dick and Harry left,
the blue light on the mither's hand was lit.

❋

She says, Tom went. Dick went. Harry went.
It was easier for Dick who was tall,
suited his clothes, a Dapper Dan, presented himself—
he worked as the corner man in a vaudeville show.
Americans liked personality. *Put it there* went over big
and with his suit and that height,
Dick landed Maître D' in a fancy restaurant.

Dick fell in.

Everyone said they couldn't do enough for him.
Good tips. They said,

Ach, the lad did well fer ehsel over in America.
Aye, Dick wi ehs fancy new teeth.

At home, the mither beamed in her new red woollen coat
while they three raw loddies flew over the ocean. Imagine.
America. All that smart chat, just like you see in the pictures.
Ach, the variety.
The selection on the shelves.

   The *get up an go.*

One day after work Dick went out the back way
and was never seen again (murdered – for his tips).
No one really knows how he got lost but he was found
in a river no one had heard of:

   the Hudson.

Back home Sam the head of the family put the phone down,
then picked it back up again and called Harry in New York.

   Yer comin haime right noo.
   An bringing Tammy wi yeh.

But Harry, in his new fly chat, said:

   No can do.

Sam put the phone down. Dust fell slowly back home
in the living room sun, first time in months.
The room filled with it. Sam closed his eyes.

   Small world it is.
   An tha silly sun oan all days as this.

Back in New York, Harry felt bad. He was just a kid.
He knew you didn't move to America to dwell on things
and if back home you're killed going out the front door,
in America you're killed going out the back way,

>this was no matinee.

No Nelson Eddy. No RCMP walking out of the Canadian evergreens.
No Fraser River you learned about in school,
but a brother, gone.

Harry in New York put down the phone.
Got on with things.
Sam got down and prayed, and Mary,
their sister, left.

※

You think, Mary's there. Mary with her good heart and head.
Mary in her brick Bronx bedroom. Visiting Mary went like this.
You'd knock, then hear her walking down the hall saying,

>Just a minute!

Unlocking bolts and turns,

>Just a minute!

Unhinging chains and locks and ties,

>Just a minute!

Finally she'd shove the big dresser out the way,
the door opened, and Mary stood, smiling, saying,

>Come away! Come away!

With that black hair. The whole place smelt like chips.
To the kitchen, the red, shiny tablecloth, the kettles,
ironing boards, armchairs covered in clothes,

> red, white and blue

the look of rooms where people leave for work every day.

Outside she was just the same. Mary in those black heels,
serge suit, lapel brooch, walking down the street, back straight.
She had a way of striding, that Toibin walk,
handbag tight under her arm. She said,

> It's after three, the trade schools are oot.

And right on cue, you'd see faces peek around corners
but with Mary striding that way with her purse,
blue eyes meaning business,
they left her glittering brooch alone.

And then, even with Mary there, even with Mary all put-together,
it happened to Harry.

For a long time the story went:

> Ach. Flamin black soot came doon tha tunnel
> an choked ehm dead.
> (Ah was jist waitin oan it.)

Harry was a driver for the old New York subway, night shift.
Back home, Harry had been the one in uniform,
the one with a good job,

> no like Dick wi ehs head a way up in the clouds,
> flyin roond wi aw tha money.
> Bad fellas waitin fer ehm oot the back.

9

Ach. Wi ehs beeg reed open face an aw.

Someone said,

> It's no good over there in America.
> Tommy, Ahm tellin yehs.
> Jist look at Harry.
> Dead of emphysema.
> Doon tha hole night an day wi oot a bit ay air.
> (Jist like the coal mine.)

As if he never left.

Dick went. Harry went.
Now one left in New York not counting Mary.
Tom. Tommy, the eldest, was different.
Tall, lean, a scout leader, he wore short pants
and laughed at everything everyone said

> when eh wasnae oan ehs knees, praying.

America. He loved it over there.
But for Tommy, last one left,

> it didnae look good.

One day he asked Mary,

> What are the odds that oot of three brothers…
> what are the odds, Mary? Aw three?

Mary stood, handbag under arm, blue brooch glittering
in the afternoon sun, and told him.

10

The other Tom's father, Willie,
was in the first war, on watch, Vimy Ridge.
Stood in the middle of no man's land
beside his friend Archie Geddes,
who he looked out for, who looked out for him.
Archie's father had his head blown in two
in the same war
months before.

Willie on the battlefield, moonlight on the back of his hand,
smoked cigarettes to make the time fly, and when he lit a match
he'd say:

> Make sure yer hands donnae shake
> so yeh donnae upset the other man.
> Always keep yer hands steady fer ehm.

The faither wouldnae have said *donnae*.
Though that night, all the wouldnae, couldnae,
shouldnae, didnae, hadnae, wullnae, cannae,
disnae and wisnae in the world didnae matter
because just then, at the base of their post,
a shadow appeared.

> It wisnae tall
> an it didnae hae a head.

Jesus, said Archie Geddes under his breath,
while Willie turned white. Was it man or woman?
It reappeared, seemed to float just above the ground
and then it floated across no man's land where it disappeared,

> like the toot.

If it had been raining, it could have been a soldier running
from the rain, but it wasnae raining. If there had been fire,
it could have been someone ducking bullets,
but there wasnae fire. Just the two men in no man's land saying,

Tha wiz a big yin.

Willie's face went aw peelly wally.
He stood poker straight and said,

Tha wasnae a yin.

No, said Archie.

Yeh couldnae hae a square go
wi an apparition such as this.

A sight like that could make the mind wander and hours later,
Archie was still talking about it, lighting matches,
hands shaking.

Hey, Wullie, why don't yeh fling yer wallies doon there.
Kinda provoke the thing.

Willie went for a look through the mud. Nothing there.
Not even a footprint. He went back to the post and told Archie,
who stood and held his rifle in such a way
so his hands would not shake,

No point callin tha in, eh?

No, no point, said Archie.

How yeh gonnae explain te yer CO
yeh saw a figure runnin headless
through no man's land

an it didnae leave a footprint?

It could have been an apparition. They'd seen a lot of death.
It could have been a dream. But that night, at post in the middle
of no man's land, Archie asked Willie,

> Ehm,
> What are the chances
> ay a faither an son dyin in the same war
> the same way?

The night was clear and Willie said,

> Ehm,
> let me see.
> Two men...wan war.
> Same family.

He counted on his fingers, like there was a method to it.

> Ah'll tell yehs tomorrow, Archie.

The next day the battle was over.
Later someone told Willie,

> ehs two legs
> jist ran oan ahead.

> *Wan, two,*
> *wan, two.*

That could have been it. But Tommy insists.
Mary, what are the odds ay aw three brothers...?
And Mary, who remembers the faither on Vimy Ridge, says,

Jist donnae ask, Tom.
Yeh know how it is.

Oh ach, the old blue light, says Tommy.
The mither's superstition.
Cannae a fella escape?
In America they'd call tha *a coincidence,* Mary.

He stormed out the back door, jacket flying over his shoulder,
American fly chat gone,

Wull yewz aw no go away noo! The lot ay yehs!

He left Mary in the kitchen with the dripping sink
and the falling dust, and Tommy and granda Dick back home
was still talking about the all-new Tommy,
over there in America.

Sam told her over the phone,

Ach. Mary. Why did yehs let ehm go?

That could have been it. But the story goes.
Tom went out as the handsome one—
the dancer, the talker, the crooner, the kind that made people say,

Too bad. Eh could sing.

As a waiter at a private club up the Hudson River he did well

well fer Dick wi ehs tips
well fer Harry
wi ehs burnin eyes
an burnin lips

14

and at the end of the night there was drink with the other waiters,
all the champagne that was left.

 Ach. Tommy.
 Eh wasnae tall but eh had lotsa pals.

And the night they were all driving home, singing away,
that black hair in the wind (inherited from the Gallachers,
McNamaras and McNamees)
the driver hit a tree
and everyone died

 but Tom.

Forehead sliced on metal, brains burst open like a soup tin,
and when they found the wreck Tom was gone.
He just walked away. They found him in a field, sitting up
(still in his good suit). When Mary heard the news,
her voice just went. Back home, Tommy and Dick said,

 Ach. New life in America.
 Two dead – wan wi no voice.
 Wan wi no head.

In Tommy's last letter home, he said he had a toothache.
Back home that was it. Show over.

 No more ay this family's goan te America.
 Over the bodies ay Tom, Dick an Harry.

When it was all over, someone said,

 Wan thing Ah'll say aboot America:
 it may be violent
 but they know how tae look after their dead.

II

The areas within the four right angles formed
by the crossed swords are termed 'spaces.'

And the other Tom, Tammy, Gallacher's brother.
Not as dramatic (but nonetheless). Tom's brother Willie,
who was tall, left for the front at Union Station in Glasgow;
the whole family went to see him away.
Willie had that black hair like the highlanders,
and in a uniform,
　　　ach.
　　　Aw the women were all looking over.

He had his cousin Tommy's teeth. Granda Dick's cheekbones.
He played violin.

　　　The mither said,
　　　Willie. You'll play the violin on yer maw's deathbed.

At the station Willie took Tom aside and told him man to man,

　　　Tom.
　　　Between you an me brother.
　　　Ah know Ahm never coming back.

For a second they stood smoking, eye to eye, Tommy holding it in.
Like Jimmy Cagney in *Angels Wi Wee Dirty Faces*.
He already knew the rest. So he said,

Don't tell meh, Wullie.
Let's jist leave it like this.

Poor Tom. One minute smoking a cigarette
with your best friend,
and the next.

The one who left.
And the one who left.

The maither dabbed her eyes and God knows Willie
waved his arm outside the train and she waved back
with that white hanky right to the end of the railway bend.

And that could have been it.
Later when two soldiers showed up at the door

clock ticking
dust falling

everyone in the neighbourhood heard.
The maither fell to her knees,

Gallacher jist screamed.

Someone said in the last months of the war,
they sent all the Scots in. The Glasgow Highlanders.
That night the father's hair turned white in his sleep.

Willie. Who suited his clothes.
He always knew what to say.

Played the violin.
Brave.

The way he left that day.
Tall.

※

Going back, when Gallacher, Tom's sister was born,
everybody thought it was going to be a boy
because the maither felt a pounding in her ribs
so hard she couldn't sleep. They laughed,

Ach. The wain jist couldnae wait.

They named her for her faither's maither, Grace Gallacher.
Born the same year as Rhapsody in Blue her eyes were blue
and she had a lively laugh, liked to play marbles, kick cans,
shoot peas, ride bikes

in a blue dress
down Glasgow hills,

a backdrop of smokestacks. Clydebank. She kept going
even when the lights came on in Glasgow winters
at two in the afternoon, well into Advent,
she wheeled round the town, down hills in the wind,

free.

The radio was always on.
American big bands followed you through
windows where people scrubbed at low sinks and no matter
where you went you could hear an American croon.
But Gallacher wanted something bigger than big bands.
She wanted to be a tap dancer. A real one.
Swords and jigs were good for the living room
but it wasn't what she wanted to be,

where she wanted to dance,
who she wanted to meet: Fred and Ginger.

Cheek to cheek.
Tomato tomahto.

Eleven years old, Gallacher took one look at Glasgow,

Ach.

Smokestacks couldn't compete with top hats and tails,
red shoes, long gowns and dancing on ceilings
when the ceiling itself dripped. When the dust fell no matter
how much you cleaned. Hard to compete with easy smiles
and lighthearted feet when every woman in Glasgow had blisters
and bunions from wearing cardboard Kitty Kelly's,

wartime shoes
always too tight.

When it came to feet, the faither was another story.
Never had a corn. Nice high instep. Beautiful feet—
he was the only man in Glasgow who had a pair of shoes
in *Toney Red*

while

the mither hobbled doon the road
wi tha hard step.

Gallacher dreamed. She did. She never missed a Fred picture
at the theatre on Sauchiehall Street. She took it all in.
At night she could hardly sleep
thinking about Fred
and those feet of his never stopped moving.

Aw they moves:
the soft shoe, the high kick, the twist, the slip,
the leap,
the rumba, samba, schottische,
the shim-sham, bombershay and Oh,

the dip.

He wasnae tall, Fred.
But he had what it took nonetheless.

Looking down from the screen with that smooth grin eyes
and chin, he had a look that said,

Start again.
Why, just pick yourself up. C'mon!

And Gallacher thought,

Ach. Eh is lookin right at me.

Oh, to dance with Fred was all she dreamed.

To waltz out of there!
To dance on ceilings!

And one day, it happened.
The maither saved up coupons for dance lessons,
no more dancing in the kitchen pretending it was Hollywood,
no, it would be real, now, right here, and Gallacher thought,

next stop: Fred.

The day of the first lesson they went down the street to the dance school.
Gallacher in a dream,

oh, light as air

in her blue dress with her mither, they flew down the hill
past a workman tapping on brick.

It was quick.

When they walked in someone said
it was not the first day of school,
but the last,
        Ach.
They stared a minute.
Teachers and students were leaving for the season.

See you next year!

Gallacher eyes were full to the brim
and the mither's eyes were full to the brim
and what else,

        what else

but to just walk back home, uphill, past the workman
who looked different than he did on the way in

        less hopeful
        like the sky

different with disappointment. The sound of chipping brick.

Jist get through it,

Gallacher thought, walking up the hill.
Jist get through

the dripping sink,
the falling dust,
the different sky.

✕

At St. Paul's school, Shettleston Road, no one could ever remember
whether Walter Bowdy was in grade three for five years
or grade five for three years.
He started at the front of the class,
worked his way back
to the end,
year by year, row by row,
he got bigger,
but never moved ahead.

Slumped, chewing on a pencil,
he just waited for the strap,
like a lot of kids in Glasgow: waiting, staring, chewing, slumped.
Tall and lanky, he towered over everybody. Tom remembers

      eh used tae hold oot ehs arm fer the teacher
      an she'd say te turn ehs arm roond the other way
      so the soft side's oot. Then tha wooden ruler would come doon
      an Walter had tae count oot the strokes
      because eh wasnae good at math.

      Wan, two, three, four, ach;
      eh never did learn tae count.

St. Paul's, Shettleston Road. Walter Bowdy was just the start.
Students punched students in the stomach all day,
no one noticed.
In fact, someone said,

Someone hits yehs an then the whole class stood up tae sing,
What do yehs do wi a drunken sailor?

Like nothing happened.
There were hand motions to go with the song.
They sang right through the wooden ruler
and the stomach punches.
Parents too scared to speak up.

Tha ruler came oot every day. Yeh were strapped fer
whispering while yeh walked up te communion
whispering while yeh walked back fre communion
thinking aboot whispering while walking up tae, back fre,
communion. It was jist the beginning.
Never mind confession, penance, Advent, Lent,
er looking oot the windae.
Ye werenae allowed tae look oot the windae.

It happened to Gallacher. What she did

wasnae missin communion, confession,
wasnae lingerin in the sweets section during Lent—
still the teacher said,
Ye might as well jist spit in Our Lord's face.

No,
it wasnae thinking aboot ice cream during Holy Week,
wasnae playin kick-the-can on a Sunday—
still the teacher said,
Ye might as well hae been the Romans dividing up tha robe.
Priests, sisters, brothers, teachers, they were all in on it,
looking doon at they raw wains, thinking,

Ye wee satanic replicas.

Never mind no givin someone who received Holy Orders
yer seat oan the streetcar, ach.

Ye might as well hae hammered in the nails yerself.

What Gallacher did.
During school a girl named Mamie whispered to Gallacher,

Do yeh wanna play marbles after school?

And Gallacher didn't even turn her head. Didn't say a word.
Didn't move a muscle. Did not flinch. The teacher looked up,
and knew. A question had been asked. And Gallacher was pondering
it.
Like a prisoner, imagining escape.
Marbles were only the start of things.

Gallacher!

the teacher said, and Gallacher, all knobby knees and blue dress,
went to the front.

Arm!

And Gallacher held out her arm.

Other way!

Gallacher turned her arm to the other side, the soft side,
then looked straight into the teacher's eyes,

steady. (No goan fer it.)

The teacher looked back, surprised.

Ah'll gie yehs a clout ye cheeky wee lassie.

CRACK

came down the ruler
and Gallacher did not flinch.

CRACK

came down the ruler again and Gallacher did not move,
not even after five times on the soft side. Not even after ten
on that same soft side. The classroom door was open.
Lizzie, her sister, passing by, went straight home
and told the mither,

> Ah saw Gallacher gettin the ruler in school.
> The door wiz open.
> She didnae flinch.

When the maither heard this she stood up,

> Ahm no standin fer tha!

And she put on her coat

> an walked stiffly doon the road
> wi tha hard step.

When the maither arrived at school

> she charged doon the hall
> went straight te the classroom,
> right up tae tha teacher.

> What's goan oan here?
> Yeh hit ma lassie wi a ruler?

The teacher stared.

Wull yer no gaunny dae tha again.

Said the mither.

No. Yer nae gaunny hurt any ay they children as long as Ahm
aroond.

The mither's eyes held the teacher's like a seat on a swing.

Jist in case ye didnae hear, the mither said.
Yer no gaunny do the likes ay tha again.
Er. Else.

Then the mither flew oota there
leavin the teacher
an aw they kids
wi their mooths
wide open.

The ruler stopped. The teacher put it away. For good.
From then on when the teacher measured distance,

she used a wee string.

Someone said,

No tha any of us wiz goan anywhere.

✳

On Shettleston Road there was a church on one side,
a school on the other, and a graveyard nearby, good for playing in.
After school they skipped marbles between the headstones,
watched them bounce off the iron railings,

runnin and skippin amongst the dead. Ach,
Glasgow was a great place for a kid.

One day the faither told them,

Tha graveyard is haunted.

During World War One, some soldiers were walking down the road
past the tall iron gates. The men were drinking,

werenae thinkin tae clearly, an wan said,
Think there's ghosts here, Jim?

And Jimmy said,

Sam, there's no ghosts. An if there wiz,
ah wouldnae be scared ay it.

Ach! Jimmy went oan te say.
Come an get me if yer man enough,
yeh wee ghosties!
An aw the men laughed.
When the laughin died doon, wan gets an idea.

He says,

Jimmy, if yehs'r no scared,
yehs'll sleep in tha graveyard tamorra night.

Ahm no scared, says Jimmy.
Ahm no scared but it doesnae mean
Ahm gaunny dae it.

Aye, it does, says the wee taunter.
If yeh were scared

yeh wouldnae
an yer no gaunny so tha means:
yer scared.

No, it disnae. Says Jimmy.
There's aye a difference between no daein it and bein scared.
Use yer head.

The challenge was oot.

Always somewan goadin yehs oan, Jimmy thought.

So the next night Jimmy goes to sleep, was snoring away
beside a big headstone when all of a sudden he hears an eerie voice
and rattling chains

jist the other side ay tha stone.

Ohhhhh but it's cold! it says.
Ohhhhhh but it's colllld! it says, louder.

Jimmy was aff like the toot.
Headed fast fer they big iron gates.

The gates were locked, bolted shut,
but he was running fast, gathering steam,
eerie voice and rattling chains behind him,
and he shouted one last time:

God gie me legs!

before he leapt. No one could believe it.
Jimmy cleared that iron gate by two feet.

Adrenalin, someone said.

A couple happened to be walking past the graveyard eating fish and
chips and when they saw Jimmy sailing over the gates,
they threw their fish and chips up in the air,
including the newspaper.

An ach. The wee taunter was oan the other side ay the street
goan,

Wull, eh did it. But did yeh see ehm run.
Eh wiz scared after aw. Ah jist knew it.

Imagine. Even after Jimmy
scaled the walls of that graveyard by two feet.

That wiz Scotland, said the faither.
You jist couldnae get ahead.

No matter the direction, someone said.

✳

Fourteen years old, Gallacher's first job
was working for a chimney sweep.
There was a wooden hut in the middle of the lane
with room for one chair.
She took appointments,
wrote them in a notebook hanging by a nail.

It wasnae much of a job

but she loved it because alone, in the coal dust,
she could read.
She loved to read.
Any book that looked good and she loved fairy tales.
It all sounded great to Gallacher.

Up and down the lanes a woman named Bridget sang
after dinner wrapped in a shawl. She had a lovely voice.

She walked up an doon an
poot aw the babies te sleep

and every so often you'd hear

the clang ay a shilling
tossed oot the windae.

Ach. Glasgow. Always the same. And Gallacher knew

it aye creeps in.
You'd be there forever if ye didnae watch.

She tried to sleep. She wondered if anyone who went to America
lived. And as Bridget went up and down the lanes, someone said,

It's no tha she really has a lovely voice,
it's jist tha her voice sounds better as she moves away.

Ach. Glasgow. Always the same. When the faither told her,

Donkeys born blind in the coal mine never leave,

she stared at the ceiling,
couldnae sleep.

III

While dancing over or across the swords
the head may be slightly inclined to allow
the dancer to see the swords.

The faither always worked in jobs where he wore a hat and uniform:
tram driver, machine man, milk delivery, ice cream sales.
But he wouldn't wear a hat, he refused because, as he said,

Men that wore hats lost their hair.

He said,

Did yeh ever notice tha men with no hair always wear hats?
Ahm tellin yehs, *it's they hats.* Stay away fre them.
A head needs air. Needs te blow in the breeze.

The faither was always particular about himself.
He would go on about hats, hair, and shoes,

women and wains lookin oan.

But, over there, there's a way of looking at men.

Mithers wring their hands
run after the faithers
wi trays ay tea an chips

always runnin oot an in,

the faithers
like customers who never leave, ach

mithers either workin
or waitin oan the next shift,

always looking after things, every dish, dog,
floor an faither.

But if things didn't suit the faither he'd say so
and after Willie went to war
everyone was running after him. He'd say,

Mither. More tea!
There's a hole in me sock. Mither!

And if she was too long, he'd start coughing.
The wiff of mustard gas he got in the war.

Mither, where's ma sweet?
Button missing. Mither!

Running in circles, pipe, slippers, neeps,
no one making a peep, the mither
putting a blanket on his knees,

There yeh aye go, faither. There y'are noo,

and Gallacher heard it all from upstairs,
the mither running after the faither and one day she thought,

No more blaither.

Standing upstairs in tap dance shoes,
she knew a few moves. She walked down the stairs,
made every third step count, just like Fred,

ratta-ra-tatta!

And everyone was there: Tommy poured tea,
Lizzie changed the radio switch, mither sliced a jam roll,
the faither in his chair in a room thick
with the smell of chips and grease,
smoke rising to the ceiling, dust falling,
and from the staircase Gallacher looked right at him and said,

Da. Don't shout at me mither again.

Tom looked from behind the teapot, Lizzie stood, blinking,
the mither held her knife in midair.
The fact she said 'don't' and not *donnae*
made everyone stop and stare.

And the faither, Ach.
His mouth dropped, his gums gaped.

Then the radio went on. The tea got poured.
The cake was cut and back upstairs, Gallacher thought,

How small the living room is.
Ah never noticed tha before.

But from then on the faither didn't shout.
Everyone could hear Gallacher's feet tapping up there,

ta-ta, ta-ta.

✳

Glasgow. Scotland. It crept in.
The faither's faither, Dick, was over six feet tall,
worked fourteen years in a mine shaft,
with a clearance of three feet.

When he laughed he threw his head back.

They all went to the mines: Tommy, Willie, Dick.
For a while the faither worked at John Brown shipyards
building the Queen's ships. He had the top mechanical job
but then someone brought in a relative for less money
and someone said,

> It wiz never good tae hae the top mechanical job.

The faither ended up houking in the mines, taking the coal out.
Below ground, the faithers faither, tall, was a top man.
When Dick went to the mines he knew by instinct
where solid ground went weak, they said,

> Eh had a gift fer seams.

There were explosions and gas leaks. Men disappeared.
People looked. No one found anyone.
The wives would be waiting outside for a paycheque.
Dick said in the mine it was one thing after another.

For Willie, it all struck deep. He took pride in it.
Someone said,

> Say what yeh like aboot the faither,
> eh always looked the part. Pure statesman.

And though he worked in the shipyards and in the mines,
he knew something better was just waiting for him.
Tall, that long straight nose, black hair,
and when he wasn't underground he carried a cane,
always polishing his toney-red shoes.

During the war the English officers noticed the faither.
They saw something in him.
One morning on the front lines,
the general called him into his tent and said,
in proper English,

even a way oot there,

said,

Tubbin. Would you like to be my *bat*-man?

The faither stood before the general,
no idea what a bat-man was.

So the faither said,

Yes, sir.

Turned out a *bat*-man was the soldier
who pressed the general's clothes and ran errands.
To the faither it was an honour. Top job.
He said,

Did yeh ever notice how they always gie the job
te Scots or Irish men?
Because the English see something in them.

Every morning the general would call him in and say,

Tubbin. Go out and describe the sky to me.

And the faither would say,

Ehm. Yes, sir.

And wonder,

How dae yeh describe the sky?

So every day the faither went out,
ducked shells,
ran through trenches,
looked up at the sky,
and returned with the same answer:

Mostly grey, sir!

One thing you can say for the faither,
he always had an answer to things.
Always a scheme on the go.
Always a way out. A plan.

Before the war he learned from an Italian neighbour
how to make ice cream, even leased a machine,
sold ice cream in the street, it tasted good,

until eh went oot oan ehs own.

Instead of sugar he used salt
of course,
and outside the football park
people were dropping their cones
all the way up and down the sidewalk.
Someone else was selling ice cream further along
and someone heard someone say,

Donnae go tae tha wan.
Go tae the wan further doon.

Still the faither stayed there all night,
and everyone said,

    Say what yeh like.
    In the end the faither got rid ay it.

It was better when the war started.
The faither got a solid job
and the family moved to a brand new housing scheme,
first time with indoor plumbing, ach.
No more door at the end of the lane,

    no more chanty-po.

A separate dining room, a good home.
You had to know someone to get in.
On moving day, Tom and two other fellas
were moving the piano up the street,
but the other fella was doing all the work
and there's Tom, hand resting on the piano.
Said he was there for moral support.
And the whole time the mither was in the hospital
with pneumonia, it was the move she couldn't wait for

    aw they years dreamin
    of good lighting. Indoor toilets. Ach.

So Gallacher was in charge,
cooking dinners, doing the washing,
and women across the road offered to help,
they had washing machines,
but Gallacher just took out the old washboard and scrubbed.
She loved to scrub, washing clothes, floors were the best,

workin alone, singin *hmm, mmm, mmm,*
up to her elbows in brushes and suds, she said,
A machine jist isnae the same.

One of the woman said she had a son named Patrick
and Gallacher just kept scrubbing, *hmm, mmm, mmm.*
The mither returned from hospital and knew
life was better, even good,

> though neighbours still keeked oot curtains.

And Patrick's mither told the mither
that Patrick had a notion of Gallacher.

> Patrick wisnae tall but
> eh wisnae wee either.
> Lovely clothes. Nice manners.
> Always comin over.

Except whenever he came over, there was the faither
giving him a staring look. Not speaking.

> Poor fella.
> The faither's family. They straight noses, tha bit,
> where somewan's still mad aboot a tray ay sandwiches
> offered tae late, twenty years ago.

> *Sandwiches.*
> Tha look wiz meant te say.
> *Ah wonnae forget they sandwiches.*

A matter of pride, the faither would say,
while the mither said,

> A matter ay bread and butter.

The faither said,

A young man moochin aboot wullnae do.

And all the while the mither knew:

Life was good
up on a hill with a water view,
of sorts. Their ship came in.

Months passed.
Patrick's older sister married someone named Willie
and since Gallacher wasn't allowed to go out with Patrick,
the mither told Gallacher,

Ach, jist meet wi aw three,

and soon the four were best friends.
With Patrick and his sister and Willie coming over,
and with working windows, indoor toilets and

Oh, a light switch,
It iz jist like heaven,

the mither said.
Until the faither stepped in.

Annie, he says one day. We're leavin.
No, the mither says. Ahm no leavin.
Annie, we're aye leavin.
No. Ahm no goan.

Annie, he says. We're goan tae England.
Ah had a letter from meh sister Lizzie askin us tae go doon there.
There's a scheme te raise pigs.

A real plan.
Ach, no, says the mither.
Ach, aye, says the faither.
An this one's a winner.
The mither thought, not another scheme.
Tam's latest one was working for the English
in the North of Scotland
picking seaweed. It was top secret. They said,

Great medicine fer the troops. Jist great.

After the war
they found oot
it wiz the wrang seaweed.

Someone said,

Ach. Good thing they didnae kill aff the whole army.
Aye. Yeh didnae need the Germans.

Oh, they were mad. But there was something to the English.
Always so confident, even without a plan.
They knew how to carry themselves, all smooth.
And while the letters went back and forth
between Lizzie and Willie about the pigs,
it started to look good.

But the mither. Leavin tha nice kitchen,
never mind, ach, the toilet bowl.
The good life didnae last long, the mither knew.

It was time to leave Scotland.
And when the last day arrived,
everything packed and ready to go,
the faither sat on the mither's kitchen chair wondering
if it was the right move.

They couldnae believe it.
Yeh might as well hae been pullin eh's teeth oot.

The mither said,

Leave yer faither alone noo.
Eh's deep in thought.

But what he was thinkin, he couldnae say.
He couldnae say because
all the while he had the family thinkin,

this was it, about to hit it big,

he was thinking about Tom, Dick and Harry.
A way over there.

Murdered or opened like a soup tin. The old ghost.
Look what happened when you stuck your foot out.
And all the while he sat on the mither's chair
fancy dressed in his two-toned shoes, red and black,
ready for England, beside the dripping sink,
all the faither could think was,

I'm a fucking Scot,

over and over again.

✳

Auntie Lizzie said the faither always had a way with numbers.
Lizzie, landowner, was the faither's eldest sister

an she didnae say much
but when she spoke ye listened.

When they all walked in she took one look at Gallacher and said,

Are you girls going to the church dance tonight?
No, they said. No dress te wear.
Right, she said.

And on the spot she got the cloth and made two flowered dresses.
She knew how to make things fit.

She had that Toibin back, tall and straight.
She walked so stately down the street, head held high,
while her husband

John Lennon

raised chickens in the house.

There were great things ahead. And the pigs.

Out in the barn, everyone there, the faither took out a pencil and
wrote:

Six pigs. Thirty-six piglets. Thirty-six pigs hae thirty six piglets
an we're up te…two hundred an sixteen piglets!
They all stared while the faither handed round the paper,
all the eyebrows flying up in the air as it passed,

Ach. Eh's got it doon.

Aw the wains an cousins said,

Rich aff pigs. Imagine!
Oozin in wealth! said one of the English cousins.
Rollin in it! said one of the Scottish cousins.

The faither knew this was better than milk delivery,
better than seaweed, better than ice cream,
better than the mine, the shipyards, or even being
a *bat*-man.

Even better than pickin up chairs wi eh's teeth.

Everything was right this time.
They set up the pen, brought in mud, built a fence,
and Tom set to work.
Everyone said he had a way with pigs
while Tom said,

They're aw brains.

There was a cousin Tom's age, Lizzie's son
(Gallacher's faither's eldest sister's son), Tom.
He was born the same day as Tom
and when the mither didn't have the milk,

Auntie Lizzie had enough fer two. Ach.

One stayed in Scotland, the other to school in England,
and the same time Tom was making a name for himself
with the pigs, the other Tom was going to university in London.
Someone said,

Makes ye wonder.
Oor Tam oot there in the mud
wi that other wan drivin past, oot the gate.

But it wasnae like tha. Ach.
Sometimes it jist wasnae.

As the mither said,

They aw make their way.

And everyone liked Lizzie's son Tom.
After university he became an officer in the British army,
a Scottish regiment in England

    an wi aw they brains

he ended up a teacher, then taught in the university.
At night, he and his brother John and other educated folk
gathered in Lizzie's living room to discuss educated matters,
science and philosophy,

    while a chicken passed the doorway
    followed by the faither.

John Lennon poked his head in the hall now and then,

    You lads awake?

Tommy thought it was great:

    Mud in ehs nails, an aw.
    Good fer they fellas.

Tom knew,

    Ye cannae feel sorry fer yerself. Ye jist cannae.
    Because once yeh start there could be no end tae it.
    Yehs could go te seed.
    Yeh could slip.

So he waved to the fellas in the armchairs,
and the fellas waved back. And Tom thought,

    Harry Lauder.

Keep right oan til the end ay the road.

And the big day arrived: Day of Birth. DOB.
Thirty-six pigs. Just like it said on paper.
Thirty-six pigs! The call went out.
They all ran down to the barn:

> Tams, Lizzies, Willies, Annies, Sams, Johns,
> Agnes, Gallacher, a Dick and two Harrys.

They stood in overalls and aprons, waiting.
Someone said,

> Ach. This wiz the way tae live.
> No livin in books like Tammy a way over there

and Tommy agreed,

> Aye, this is it.
> Eh had tae admit.
> Yeh couldnae beat this.
> Real life.

Today the other Tom was centre stage,
in position to bring in thirty-six pigs,
the faither stood beside Tom with a pencil
ready

> te take doon aw they numbers.

They held their breath. And the faither solemnly
held up his fingers for the first tally:

> Wan.
> Hurray! the shout went up.
> The first, the lucky one!

Everyone was shouting and slapping each other on the back.

Ha! someone said.
The faither's gaunny get ehs fingers worn oot
indicatin aw they numbers!

They laughed again and waited for more.
Thirty-six. At least!

Ach no, said the faither.
Yehs have tae be realistic. Thirty-six.

They all agreed.

Thirty would be alright tae, added the faither.

They all nodded. Thirty would be alright too.

They waited. They held their breath.
With a very solemn expression,
the faither held up his finger again, indicating

one.

Ach.

The same one. A sigh filled the room.
And everyone agreed,

we'll settle for ten.

A few moments later the faither looked up,
all serious, and held up his finger once more.

Jist the wan.
Wull, someone said. These things aye take time.

Tae right, Wullie. Yeh cannae rush nature.

By this time the neighbours were all there,
a crowd gathered at the door of the barn
while Wullie held up his finger,

Wan,
jist the wan

enough times that finally everyone fell quiet.
Finally Tom brought out the one

jist the wan

and they all stood and looked.

Jist the wan, the faither said.

The pig stood blinking, small and pink.

Ach, Tom said.
Yeh cannae get tae upset.
Jist look at ehm.

It was quiet in the barn. Someone said,

But ehs no much is eh? Still an aw.

And they all fell in,

Ach, no.
No, it isnae.
Kiddin oan it didnae really matter in the first place
after aw tha hard work
buildin fences an feedings.

The faither said,

> Ach. No. It didnae matter.

And after a while someone said,

> Course, it would be tha bad
> if we wiz expectin somethin tae begin wi.

They all fell in,

> Ach. That's right.
> Good thing we wusnae!
> It aw worked oot fer the best. Aye.
> Jist what we expected!

And someone said,

> Still an aw. It's no much – is it?
> And they jist stared. An fell silent again.
> An sometimes yeh aye wonder, thought the faither.

That night the faither said to the maither,

> *No much is it.*
> Aw they folk standin roond watchin
> what other people are aye doin
> an no doin.
> Ye donnae see *them* stick their neck oot!
> Even aw though, thought the faither.
> Yeh wonder.

The next day Tom put a sign on the barn,

> *Closed,*

and the other Tom drove past, and waved,

and drove oot the gate.

And all Tom could think was

fre six pigs te thirty-six pigs
te two hundred an sixteen pigs
how dae yehs end up wi jist wan?
Jist the wan?
Two hundred and fifteen, mind, less,
than what yehs were expectin
in the first place?

He bet even his cousin Tom
didn't have the answer for that.

IV

The amount of turn at the end of each step
is determined by the starting position
of the step which follows.

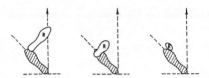

The day the war started, the family moved to Folkestone.
Down the road Gallacher and her sister walked
and saw the front page of the newspaper

WAR DECLARED

and they stood and looked at the other shore
and waited for the planes.

There was a gathering of men.
Turns out, the British weren't really ready after all.
They put the army together with great imagination
and even the faither with his wiff of mustard gas
from the first war was asked to step in.
The officer gathered them round.

> Men. Right. We've got a job ahead of us.
> England needs able bodies for service.
> A chance to show our mettle. Do you follow me, men?

This was alright by the men,

> Aye, let's show Jerry!

The officer said,

Who knows anything about explosives?

The men stood. Most of them hadn't worked in years.
But the faither, dressed in green felt trousers,
had worked in the mines.

Ehm....he cleared his throat. Ah do, sir.

They all turned and looked,

Who's this?

Bill, you are in charge, said the officer.

He gave him a crew of two men, and left.

Now the faither wasnae too sure of himself.
This was the British army and he knew
underneath they were all business.

The faither was expecting to be at the front lines again,

heedless ghosts or no.

As someone said,

Wan thing Ah'll say aboot the faither
eh always landed oan ehs feet.

The next day at midnight, the faither and his crew
met the officer and a junior man at a hangar
full of cannon shafts: the faither couldnae believe his eyes.

Turns oot, they guns werenae real.
Turns oot, they were just old painted telegraph poles.

The junior man said that the Germans would fly over
and get an eyeful. The faither and his crew nodded.
Painted telegraph poles made to look like guns,

Noo, this was a plan the faither could appreciate.

The plan was top secret so the faither could not tell the family
where he was going every day and when he left for work
in the mornings, he'd tell the mither
in his important voice,

a voice that didnae encourage questions,

Mither. Ah am goan oot.

From her kitchen chair she'd calmly say,

Oh, aye. We'll see yeh later noo.

And as the faither walked down the road to meet the other fellas
each morning, he thought to himself,

Wan thing Ah'll say aboot the mither,
she's a hard wan te impress.
But once she finds oot the part Ah played in aw this.

The faither's secret mission was to blow big deep holes for the poles

in the White Cliffs ay Dover. An it wasnae easy.
Yeh had te know what yeh were daein.
So yeh didnae blow up the whole shoreline.

You had to make a hole just big enough for a telegraph pole.

So there wiz the faither,
goan up an doon the cliffs ay Dover
in charge, like the faither's faither, Dick,
an ehs faither Tommy,
and he knew jist where te look

fer the cracks.

An wan day, the faither doon the hole,
wan ay the men said,
Bill. Germans.

You could hear them overhead.
The faither and the man waited for the bombs
but the bombs never came, not the next day
or the next and everyone agreed,
seeing those long guns, hundreds and hundreds,
the Germans left.

Aye. The faither did his bit.

The faither he told the mither he had news,
she better sit down. The faither told the whole story,
left nothing out, said the English had entrusted to him
a top secret project.
To save England.
He might even have ended the war itself.

The mither nodded, Oh aye.

The faither thought he'd take advantage of this
and go to the pub for a wee while. On his way out he said,

Ach. An it wasnae easy makin sure yehs didnae blow up
they Cliffs ay Dover so they all didnae come doon, toon an all.

Oh aye, said the mither.

The door closed. The faither walked down the street wondering
if the mither heard him correctly. He thought,

She's aye a hard wan te impress.

The mither went over
to the kitchen window
to peel potatoes,

an kep an eye oan they cliffs.

※

They moved to London.

WAR DECLARED

Yeh didnae need dance lessons fer this, ach.
Yeh didnae need te save a thing.

WAR DECLARED

Gallacher an her sister went intae a world
ay foxtrots, crooners and service men.

WAR DECLARED

And it was quick.

The Germans caught on about the telegraph poles
and one day, war on everyone's lips,

Gallacher was walking home
and saw the Anderson shelters set up in every third backyard or so,
metal domes the shape of subway tunnels and someone said,

It's gettin close tae haime.

Makes yeh wonder if Tam, Dick and Harry
werenae safer over there.
We're aw gaunny end up
wan oan top ay the other
in tha thing.

Some were stubborn, pretended to be brave.

Ahm no gaunny go intae tha thing.
No. Ahm no goan doon there, ahm no settin foot.
Ach. Ah'd rather die in meh own bed.

But when the sirens wailed,

they aw went doon, sat face te face,
aw the bravado gone.

Gallacher told the mither she wasnae goan doon there
wi aw they ants

and after the first siren, Gallacher and the mither opened the back door
and went straight in. You could hear the *ping ping* on the metal roof
and Gallacher covered her head, flew to the ground, her face right up
to the ants, praying. Someone said,

Wan thing Ah'll say aboot the war,
there were a lot ay conversions.

Two and a half years, always at mealtime,

Yeh heard the siren, went oot the door,
ping ping oan the roof, it got te be routine.
Yeh even got te know which planes were flyin overhead:
allied spitfires made a whirring sound,
like a mechanical ceiling fan.
Yeh were glad te hear it, it made yeh feel safe,

while the Germans were deep,

whoooah....WHOOOOAH....whoah,
yeh could feel it in yer heart an chest.
Yeh got te know the difference.

No matter the sound, no matter the plane,
people held on to St. Anthony's medals,

prayed to the patron saint of lost things
so the Germans wouldnae find them.

Ping ping on the roof, once so bad everyone was making deals,

God, if yeh let me live Ah will
not miss mass
an stop takin the Lord's name in vain.

Someone said,

God, Ah'll stop aw tha fuckin swearing, Ah swear Ah will.
An *God if Yehs let me live Ah will...* wiz aw ye heard.
Aw they lapsed Catholics came runnin back,
promisin, while the Germans advanced,
te stop this er tha.
Desperate deals made oota fear.

Doon in the shelter wi the noise, the ants,
holy medals an rosary beads,

jist when you thought
it couldnae get worse ye heard,
God if yeh let me live Ah will....

And once in London when they left the shelter,
the whole block, every house, was gone – except theirs.
She saw a quilt stuck in a tree, waving at them.

God, if Yeh let me live Ah will
wiz aw ye heard,

promise and sin
between the whir and ping,

you got to know the difference.

The government sent a letter:
everyone had to make sacrifices for the war effort.
So Gallacher left school, went to work,
and the mither said,

Yeh can always go back te it.
(The faither didnae say a word.)

In 1940, she went to work at the soda pop factory in Sheriton,
a red brick building above the railway: sixteen years old,
grey uniform, hairnet, she worked alone all day in a big factory room
surrounded by clear tubes, metal cans and glass bottles.
She worked in the dark, lights out to save money,
always half expecting a face to appear around the corner.
All day alone with the factory sounds,

Phhhh. Phhssssss!
Phhhh. Phhssssss!

All in grey she stood behind factory windows
thick with soot and her job was to pour red and green
syrup into bottles winding along a conveyer belt,
steady as a train, she was told,

    this colour and this colour make this drink
    an this colour and this colour make this drink

and she was left to it, pulling levers, and now and then
she'd stop the machines, fill the bottles with gas,
fizz rising to the surface, colourful bubbles, ach, like ocean waves,

    her favourite part
    was puttin oan the fizz.

Then the capping conveyer, stamping on caps,
the whole pop factory room had a sound of its own,

    bottles in rows,
    the red and green,
    the cap, the fizz, aw they machines
    goan aw afternoon, Gallacher all alone.

Sounded good to Lizzie, she had to have a peek,
see what she was missing. Like a kid, still at school.

    It wasnae discussed. Lizzie's number didnae come up
    an tha wiz tha. Ach. Gallacher had te dae her bit.
    It wasnae discussed.

And the day Lizzie showed up at the factory

    it didnae go well.

Gallacher told her where to stand, out of the way,

but Lizzie wasnae happy standin oot the way,
she didnae like the sound ay tha.

She tossed her big red curls,

Ach, Ah'm gaunny jist hae a look, she said.

The machinery whizzing, all very exciting, she thought,

Jist look where Gallacher gets te spend her days.

She peered in for a look at the capping machine,
and just when the machine went one way,
she took a closer, longer look,

ach,

a long twisting metal bit caught her hair,
an aw they flamin red curls slowly got pulled in

but Gallacher ran quick to the wall, flipped the switch,
the machine let go. Lizzie pulled her hair back, all safe,
her face beet red. Gallacher felt sorry for her, said,

That could ay turned yer head te raw meat.
Yeh were lucky.

But Lizzie, scared, didnae want te hear it,

Lucky! If ye'd been doin yer job right in the first place
this wouldnae ay happened at aw!

All the way home she cried. And when she ran in the door
she showed the mither and faither her tangled red curls,

Look at this! Would ye look at this! Booo-whoooooo!

But the faither said,

What were yeh daein lookin intae that machine fer?

The faither was all for Gallacher this time,
could remember the work in the sheet metal plant in Glasgow
when he'd just finished talking to Charlie Locheed.
Charlie hid his tools under one of the machines,
one that made rough metal smooth,

an it went slow one way then swung back

quick,

he was always aye hidin things, Charlie,
and when no one was lookin he climbed in,
reached doon

and the machine went slow one way
then swung back

quick.

The men jist stood.
One minute the faither wiz talk te Charlie,
the next, his face wiz gone,

torn aff.

He ran aroond the factory floor an aw the faither saw
was red, the faither said

it looked like a brilliantly coloured scarf

and even before he stopped running,
his wife was at the door

waitin oan a paycheque.

When the faither got home his face was pure white.

The faither said to Lizzie,
A good thing Gallacher wiz there te save yeh.

Down at the pop factory, alone,
pulling levers, putting in the fizz,
Gallacher looked out the milky windows,
down the hill to the train track
where soldiers passed back and forth all day.
She got used to the sight of them,
sometimes she could only see their outlines,
the windows were that dirty.

One day she took out a cloth and cleaned them,
stood on a stool, gave them a good wipe
and machines whizzing, clattering away,
she looked oot they clean windows
an saw,
for the first time in her life,

Canadians.

Ach.

Canadians were so polite.
Their train was stopped for a whole day
before they even put their noses outside for a walk.
She watched them through the windows,
on the grass, new recruits.

With the machines off she heard their voices,
clear as winter,

she'd never heard anything like it.

When she went home at night she told the others
about the Canadians, how they walked, so loose,
with uplifting laughs. Gallacher's mind raced
while Lizzie stared into the stew.

Looking through the windows,
Gallacher had a good look

at they uniforms, the colour of dry moss on trees

and the soldiers were tall. They were all tall.
And she heard them call out,

Hey! Whattaya thinka the eats?
Great. Bert. What else do ya need, eh?
Ah tell ya.

And they all laughed.
Just like that. Loose.

Gallacher couldnae get over it.
Accents yeh could trust, she thought.
An tall, mind, as trees.

One afternoon it was sunny and she took her lunch outside
with the girls from the gasworks next door.
They sat on top of the fence, what they must have looked like
in grey uniforms, hairnets left inside.
One of the fellas on the train spotted Gallacher's
high brown mantilla of curls. He scrambled up the hill.
The girls laughed, Gallacher was struck:

It's Joel McCrea wi tha blond lock
hanging doon ehs forehead.

He said,

Hello.

Jist like in the pictures.

Hello.

Things went well. They made small talk.
The Canadians were nice to listen to.
The Canadians' train had to wait,
there was a problem down the track. Gallacher thought,

Ach. In war they'd tell yeh anything.

Out the corner of her eye she saw the moss uniform and knew,

Tha uniform is goan te the front.

After that, when she looked at his face,

it didnae look the same.

She went back in, poured in the red, put in the fizz,
clamped on the caps
and thought about the front where they were all headed,

didnae seem real.
Britain so dull an grey,
hard tae imagine a front that close.

Gallacher and Joel McCrea talked a couple of times.

Eh said eh'd never been te war before
didnae know what te expect,
said he didnae really know what the front meant.

The day before he left
he brought her a package
wrapped in brown paper, tied with a string,
and inside was a blue satin pillow
with a poem he'd written on it
stiched in yellow thread and alongside it,
a framed picture of himself. He said,

> Ah brought tha pillow from Canada
> fer the first girl Ah fell in love wi.
> Well. Yer the girl.

> She couldnae believe it. *Yer the girl.*
> It wouldnae work.

Just then the soldier's face

> wi Joel McCrea's blonde lock oan tha forehead

disappeared before her eyes, replaced by

> the staring faither wi tha straight nose

the picture of the faither in her mind,
so angry it was actually speaking to her,

> Ahm telling yehs, if yeh so much as talk
> te wan ay they soldiers....

The soldier broke in,

> It's the real thing, Gallacher. Can Ah write te ye?

Ach. Such a nice clear voice too.

What could she dae but look at ehm.
Tha forehead, shiny as a beeg apple.
Blue satin pilla, good grief.

And staring down the green slope to where the train waited,
she thought,

Wan thing Ah'll say aboot they Canadians,
they know how te make up their minds.
Quick.

She didn't know what to say. So she said:

Me faither is very strict.

What was left but to run back up the hill,
back to the old red brick, back to the colours
and bubbles and fizz, back to the old and not-so-new?
There was no convincing the faither, she already knew.
For the girls war was a backdrop for love
while the faither was always shaking his head.
And the next day the train left in a trail of cheers
for the front

wi Joel McCrea an tha blond lock, ach.
Gone fer good.

It was back to the same.
Gallacher poured in the green, put in the fizz,
watched the bubbles and thought,

Ach. There iz no romance in any ay this.
Moss uniform an tha forehead. Tall. Gone.

And even though more soldiers passed below
the train never stopped again.

Gallacher watched as they passed,
Canadians and British poured into the front, full of hope,
all the noise, every now and then you'd heard a big

    Hurray!

A never-ending supply going one way
but soon the trains started returning

    half full of men
    who didnae look
    quite the same
    as they did on the way in.

Long faces, limbs gone, heads torn, shrapnel, eye injuries,
all the red-apple shine,

    an pillas, an voices, ach, all gone.

Even the trains were slower returning,
the big rush over.

Once she heard,

    Dunkirk.

While another lit a cigarette, staring back at the neighbourhoods
and chimneys, back at the red bricks and said,

    Old Blighty.

After a while, Gallacher heard the bombs fall
and she just kept on working and one day,
pouring in the green, putting in the fizz,
the gasworks next door was hit,
and all the windows in the pop factory were blown in.

Her cousin

Richard Nixon

heard about it and he jumped on his bike
and rode the whole way there to see if Gallacher was okay
and when he walked in,

>   Gallacher wasnae hurt,
>   was good as new,
>   sittin oan the floor
>   with a million tiny pieces of glass on her grey uniform.

Ach. There would be other Joel McCreas.
Maybe Canada was full of them.

※

When Tom heard

WAR DECLARED

he went straight down to enlist with his brother Willie

>   but they didnae want Tom. Heart murmur.

>   No, we cannot have that, son, the English recruiting officer said.
>   Talking to Tommy as if he was the faither,
>   and all the rest of the Scots, his sons.

>   Nice fella, said Tommy.
>   But he wondered, Heart murmur?
>   Never heard ay such a thing.

He was too shy to ask until Willie gave him a nudge.
Tom stood. The man looked up.

Scuse me, sir, Ah hate tae, ehm, yeh know, but what is
a heart *mur*-mur? Ah cannae seem te...ehm...

Speak up man! Said the officer.

Tom cleared his throat,

Ah sehd: WHAT'S A HEART MURMUR? SIR!

The room went quiet then.

A heart murmur
makes you ineligible
to join
the British army,

the officer replied.
Next!

And that was it. Tommy walked away and Willie was next.

Ach, Wullie, so quiet, so strong, tall;
he played the violin.
Aw they English jist loved Wullie.
Just the chap we're looking fer, they said.

And later, Willie burst in the door,

face aw pink, Maw, Ahm in!
Ah've joined the Glasgow Highlanders!

The mither gave Willie a hug,

Ach, mah big strong loddie!

And Tom followed, face pink too.

Ehm…said the mither, hands oan her apron.

What's this then? The faither walked in the kitchen.
Willie's in and Tommy's no in? Why noat?

Tom stood. Aw serious.

Da. Ah…Ah…'ve a heart, a heart murmur.

The faither put his ear to the side and shook his head.

Tam. Ah cannae hear a word wi aw tha mumbling.

The mither said,

A heart murmur, Willie.

And the faither said,

Ah cannae understand any ay yehs.
But Ah'll say this:
if any wan ay oors gets oota fightin fer they English,
more power te yehs.

The family stood, amazed.
First time the faither stood up for the Scots.
The times were changing.
Then the faither shook Tommy's hand and said,

Good man, Tammy.

Then he shook Willie's hand.

Good oan yeh, men. Both ay yehs.

When the faither left the room, Tammy said,

The faither'll aye surprise yehs, eh Wullie?

Everyone said,

>   Tam wasnae tall
>   but eh could tell a joke.

He got that bit from the mither's side,

>   They were aw loose, the Rodgers,
>   didnae take theysehls tae seriously,
>   while the faither's side could stop yeh in yer tracks
>   wi wan look.

Tommy was shy, dead scared,
but thought he'd make a good showman, onstage.
So he got a job at the Dennison Palais dancehall,

>   where eh wouldnae be starting oot oan stage,
>   no really dancing, mind,
>   but yeh never know it might lead te other things.

One day the family visited Tommy in Dennison at his work.

>   No much ay a place is it, said the faither.

Just then the dance floor cleared
the band struck up the "Colonel Bogey March"
and from behind the curtain appeared four men,
pushing brooms, dressed in matching grey uniforms
with round hats with wee strings under their chins

>   like yeh'd see an usher wearin at a theatre.
>   They couldnae believe it.
>   Is tha oor Tam? the mither said.

An ach. There wiz Tom, marchin wi three others, aw short,
ehs face turnin pinker an pinker,
tha Toibin head, mind, gettin redder and redder until,
between ehs face an aw they other faces,
ehs head looked like
a beeg reed sweetie.

Hard te miss.

The faither stared.

Oor Tam's the half-time entertainment?
It wiz tae much te bear.

Annie, yeh see noo, he said tae the mither.
If ye hadnae babied Tammy he'd be aff
wi oor Willie in tha war, no aw this.

The sweep finished with a grand finale, a complicated bit,

the crowd pleaser

as Tom called it, when they'd all zig and zag

wan fella windin roond the other wan
then tha fella windin roond the next

until aw the dust fre the dancers ended up
in a big pile at wan end,

where the music ended with a flourish.

Tommy came over after,

Ah didnae look tae stupid ah hope?

The faither lifted up both eyebrows.

Stupid? Ach, no Tommy.
What's stupid aboot makin a livin fer yersehl?
Ah tell yeh what's stupid: no sweepin tha floor.
Noo, tha's stupid.

Everyone agreed.
And everyone thought something happened to the faither
ever since he blasted holes in the White Cliffs of Dover.
More understanding. Affable.
But there was something else the faither wanted to know,

Eh, Tam, why are aw they fellas the same height? Ehm…
no tae tall ay fellas are they?

Tom said,

Ach aye. They donnae hae te pay as much
because we're no tall fellas.

The faither nodded.

Tha so, Tommy. Tha so.

But to himself the faither thought,

Aye. Imagine.
No payin short men the same wage as tall fellas.

Scotland. There iz no getting ahead, thought the faither.

It wiz aw tae much.

Gallacher and Lizzie were amazed
Tom went in the first place,
he was so shy. For years he ignored his sisters
when he saw them walking down the street,

    doon Sauchiehall, ach,
    when he saw them he didnae even wave,
    he jist crossed over tae the other side.

    But Tommy had someone looking oot fer him.

    Come tae think of it, thought the faither,
    if he was pushing a broom it was fer a reason,
    maybe missing oot on something worse.

One day in Folkestone
the faither and Tommy worked for the army
in 'strategy.' While the faither and the British officer in charge
stood talking, Tom offered to bring tea.
So Tommy went down the road.
On the way back, he saw the faither and the officer
standing across the field, a hundred yards away
and he thought he'd leave the road,

    take the shortcut. Ach.

The faither and the officer looked at Tom crossing the field,
balancing a tray full of teacups, brilliant red hair,
and the faither's stomach lurched:

    What's tha fella up te?

There was Tom, happy as a lark,
walking through a minefield,
balancing a tea tray.

The faither was ready tae shout,

Get oot!

But the English officer held out his arm and said in a calm voice,

No. Just let him go, William. Ah've seen this before.
It's better if you don't say anything.

Ach, they English. Such ay calm cool head.

So the faither stood, arms folded.
When Tom arrived, handed over the tea,

There y'are,

the faither took the tray,
set it down,
looked straight at Tom and said:

Tam. Yeh jist walked straight through a minefield.

And Tom slumped to the ground.

Fainted, poor chap, said the officer,
stirring milk in his tea.

That's when the faither knew
Tom would make it through,
after all.

Heart murmur or no. Even aw though:

After that his heart never murmured again.

V

Bow. Bring arms to First Position, if not already so placed.

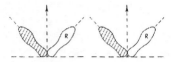

Glasgow, 1945.
After two and a half years in Folkestone,
in Glasgow the war was different.
No bombs, no jobs, and for Gallacher and Lizzie,
two years older,

    ach aye,

there were soldiers.
Now, there are highlanders a way over six feet tall

    wi tha black hair
    who come intae Glasgow
    aw handsome
    wi they eyes.

Some say they have a power that sends a shock through you
and it could be.

    Could be. We're ninety percent water after aw
    an wi tha magnetic pull,
    yeh never know, ach.

Others say,

    It's the water.

Jist look what it did fer the whiskey.
They fellas draw yehs in
walking intae Glasgow, over six feet tall, towerin above
ye wonder.
Ye wonder aboot tha water.

If the water's no workin in yer interests, ach,
it forces a local fella tae pick up chairs wi ehs teeth
jist tae get noticed and even then,
it's hard tae compete.

But in Glasgow, with the war

they highlanders got a wee bit ay competition.

Everyone said,

Overnight there were soldiers goan up and doon the road.
Ah wonder what they thought ay the wee hooses
compared tae what they'd seen in America—
what did they think ay oos?

Suddenly, soldiers, confident, swinging their arms

up and doon the road,
aw smiles, wi they fancy white teeth,
calling oot tae wan another
in they accents. Ach, aye,
American soldiers.
Glasgow didnae know what hit it.

The place to be in the middle of the day during the war in Glasgow
was the Locarno dance hall where you could dance,
have a cold drink, or a cup of tea.

It wasnae the décor,
or, ach, the food, they went fer.
It wiz jist a place tae gather,
a place tae meet.

Aw they fellas. Ye could dance wi them
wi oot getting poked in the shins
er jabbed in the knees.

Ach.

When the Americans came to Glasgow
suddenly they were all standing in the middle of a tall forest
they'd heard about in school.
When the Americans came to Glasgow

ye could keep a wee bit ay mystery because, ach,
they jist seemed above it all.

And the polite manners.

They werenae embarrassed to bring yehs something over tae eat
er drink. The Glasgow girls couldnae get over it, aw carried away
wi they accents an sayings, the way words came right oot:
Sweetheart and *Honey,*
the words jist rolled along, aw smooth, like a river
tae go wi they woods.

So optimistic,

Wanna dance?
Come on!
Right this way!
Ach, jist slidin along. Even how they danced,
they didnaes care if yeh said yehs er no,

jist goan along,
so carefree.

Even American city boys looked like country boys

wi aw tha fresh food. No eating oota tins,
no like in London wi
aw tha bad air, ach.
Lizzie's red hair use tae turn black when she came in.
Imagine yer lungs.

But aye, they soldiers.

Once Gallacher was walkin doon Union Street in Glasgow
and three soldiers passed
and wan whistled,
God bless the one that bore ya.
Aw they words, the girls loved it.

Confidence. And the thing was,

if yeh looked closely
ye could see
they werenae tha tall.

In fact,

the wan who called oot
looked jist like tha wan in Abbott and Costello.
Yeh didnae even notice, ach,
callin doon crowded Union Street in tha big voice.

The Glasgow girls werenae used tae aw tha attention.
The locals barely looked at ye, tha straight-laced;
they talked tae other fellas
when they talked at aw.

And if they wanted tae ask yehs oot
they stood fer ages, and finally ye'd get:

De ye want tae go dahncing....
or would ye like tae go tae the pictures?
Aw clipped.

And the faither would be in the door saying,

Ah donnae know what's the matter wi they fellas.

They'd run up to the door sometimes,
looking for their friends,

Is Rabbie here noo, is Rab aye in?

And the faither would say,

There is no *Rab* here. Speak proper. Say: *Robert*.

Everyone, even the faither, said,

Donnae gae oot wi a Scotsmen.

But there was always Ribbie Ribchester,
an older gentleman who showed up at the door one afternoon.
He was well off. Parents both highly educated,
he had a way with words, his favourite expression was,

Love-ely! Love-ely!

as he walked arm in arm with his lady buddies

doon Sauchiehall.
Oh no, he loved the ladies.
A wartime gent ye'd gae oot wi as a friend

but no as a date. Aye, Rabbie, he loved the Locarno.
Danced wi Gallacher and Lizzie, held his head high, so correct
wi tha straight back. He had a brother who was educated, PhD,

and at the Locarno

he jist stared at the door. Aye. They said,
Aw tha higher education went fer his napper.

And with the war on, even before they Americans arrived,
ach, there werenae tha many fellas tae begin wi.
Ye did what ye could. Jist made do.
Even the mither knew it.

Ye didnae want tae turn oot like Ludie.

Her sisters, two spinsters, Agnes and Nellie,
two teachers on Quarrybrae Street, took turns telling it:

Ludie, with her long white gloves pulled up tae the elbows,
always stylish with a little velvet hat sewn with beads
that looked like diamonds. Agnes?

She had a nice quiet fella she went out wi an he loved her
an she loved him an every night they went oot
an came back home an every night. Nellie?

She threw the engagement ring at ehm and said:
An donnae come back! Agnes?

Ludie? Ludie? Eh'd call up tae the window
an she'd slam the door every night. Nellie?

And then she'd slam the window.
Well, one night, she took the ring,
threw it at him as usual an said: *And donnae come back.*

They looked to one another, shook their heads,
serious as can be,
and said it together:

And he never came back.

Then Agnes would say:

She was a spinster all her life.

Ach. Ye didnae want to turn oot like tha.

So the mither encouraged Rabbie and others, whoever there was.

The mither said in the first war
    there were never any fellas
    so the day a fella from the parish wiz at the door, sayin,

Ah'd like tae take Gallacher tae the pictures,

she went. They went to this great big movie house downtown,
and Gallacher

    couldnae see the similarity between Nelson Eddy up on tha screen
    an this wan doon here
    and she knew it wouldnae really go tha far.

She knew there'd be a Fred Astaire, there'd be a Joel McCrea.

    Ach, there'd be a Nelson Eddy.
    Wi aw they soldiers, life would be different.
    An it wouldnae include
    a lifetime ay goan tae the pictures wi local fellas.

    With every fella, it was the same.
    Every other evening a fella from the parish would show up

at the door and eh'd stand fer ages outside

in ehs torn cuffs, imagine, before he'd finally say ehs line:

De yeh want to go dahncing....
or would ye like tae gae tae the pictures?

The mither said,

Ach, yehs've got tae get started somewhere.

She used to say,

Things are meant tae be.
And even if ye never leave the hoose,
then tha fella'll turn up oan yer doorstep.

So Gallacher went.
They went down to Sauchiehall, the two of them,
Gallacher done up in a nice skirt,

oot fer the evening while eh never even bothered
with ehs clothes, like aw they other fellas,
tae embarrassed te comb their hair,
in case ye started getting notions.

Ach, no worries there, Gallacher thought, head held high,
walking beside the parish fella slumpin along,
pickin up sticks oan the ground, pokin'em through a fence
while eh made ye stand an wait
til yeh felt yer flesh creep. Imagine.
They'd ask yehs oot
then they're tae embarrassed tae be seen oot
wi ye. The cheek.

Everyone said,

Donnae go oot wi a Scotsman.

Sitting in the theatre watching *Rose Marie*,
a popular picture, the theatre was packed for days.
Nelson Eddy and Jeannette MacDonald,
rugged Canadian peaks,

aw they lakes and rivers. So wild.
Jeannette MacDonald wi tha red hair
an they flirty eyes
while Nelson Eddy was so serious,
with ehs Canadian *Love Call*.
Ach. It wasnae Sauchiehall Street
oot wi the parish fella.

For Gallacher, seeing *Rose Marie* was it.
Last time she'd go out with any of them.
Even Jimmy Cagney in the movie trailer

wi aw ehs bravado.
An Nelson Eddy wi aw ehs manhood,
ach. What dae yeh think tha parish fella did?
Eh didnae even walk doon the stairs wi ye from the balcony.
Ach no. Might be someone doon below sees yehs
an they might start gettin notions
aboot the two ay you and that'd tie a fella doon. No.

The parish fella sat oan the top ay tha long winding brass bannister,
polished so nice fer Jimmy, Fred, Nelson, Ginger, Jeannette and
fer Humphrey Bogart, nay fer the likes ay tha unwashed parish fella

but nevertheless,

he slid right doon tae the bottom

like it was his own place.

Imagine. As if to say,
Who cares what yew think.
Pure mamas boy.
They put yeh in the position ay standin there watchin
what they're daein even if it wuznae worth lookin at.

Well, Gallacher had enough. She just walked on.

An the parish fella said,
Aw come on. Ah wis only testin it oot.
Aw fer Gawd's sake. Come back here.
Me maw's gonna gie me lalldy if Ah don't bring yehs haime.

Imagine.

Doesnae comb ehs hair. Doesnae get rigged oot.
Doesnae pay a shilling. Doesnae walk shoulder tae shoulder wi ye
doon the street. Doesnae wait fer ye tae leave yer seat because
they're tae embarrassed tae have others see ye take an interest
in a lassie. An wonnae even walk doon the staircase wi ye in case
ye started tae get notions,

an the only time he talks to yehs is when

he starts thinking aboot ehs maw being mad
cause he didnae take yehs haime.

Imagine.

So she just walked on.

After aw, someone had tae say: Enough.
Someone had tae say: Alright. And walk oan.
Head tall. Someone had tae.
If someone didnae

aw they Glasgow girls'd be standing at the bottom ay
long brass bannisters waitin oan parish fellas, while

Fred Astaire and Nelson Eddy went on ahead.

But, ach. They soldiers.
Wi the Americans it was nothin but fly chat
aboot home, barbecues and picnics,

Gallacher and Lizzie never heard the likes, even the words:

movie, cartoon, jive, baby, ach.
It wasnae real
but tha didnae matter,
they made yeh want tae stick with them
wi tha easy goan swagger,
tha bounce in their step,
jist made fer city streets,
jist made fer walking wi. Ach.

There was a war on. But something the Glasgow girls knew:

ye wouldnae, couldnae, didnae and above all: ye shouldnae
marry an American. No. Something aboot they blue uniforms,
they determined grins, they jokes an yon fly chat aboot barbecues
wiz good fer walking doon the street wi,
but no fer staying at haime wi,
because once a girl went oot wi
an American everyone knew:
ye'd never get haime at a decent time again.

Ach. They American soldiers.

Ye never married them. Even aw though
so many ay them were tall an had the chat,

the fun, jist the way they made yehs feel ˅
but even with aw tha, something wasnae right.

Something in their eyes
was wild

    an ye knew, ye jist knew
    it wasnae the water.

✖

They all loved the mither.
Standing at the door in her white apron

    bringin oot sweets and wee sandwiches,
    couldnae dae enough fer them, an ach,
    the faither didnae like tha.

    With aw they American soldiers comin roond, he said,
    Mither, will ye stop encouraging aw they yanks?
    Ahm telling yeh.
    Ah was a soldier mahsel. Ah know.

    Aye faither, said the mither. Alright faither, said the mither,
    shoooing the faither aff tae work in the mornings
    an oan tae the pub in the evenings
    tae make room fer aw they American soldiers who arrived
    in ever larger groups, the mither getting up earlier and earlier
    te make the meat pies and sweets and then they'd arrive, singin songs.

They all said:

    It feels like haime.

They'd look at the mither sitting there with her big apron,
and when they left they'd give her a big hug and say:

You remind me of my mom.
The mither jist loved it.
They reminded her ay Frederic March in *Les Miserables*.

Can Ah bring yew fellas anythin else noo? She'd say.
Yer growin loddies.

And more arrived, not just Americans but Canadians and Polish,

ach, they poor Polish sailors.
No haime tae go haime tae

even when the war ended.

Ach, they Polish fellas were thin,
so polite. They jist soaked it aw in:
jelly rolls, meat pies, sausage rolls, tea,
they didnae say much,
didnae say:
Ye remind me of my mom

because most ay they Polish soldiers
didnae have much of a haime tae begin wi.
Ach.

For Glasgow, the war brought more soldiers
and the mither found herself a mither to hundreds,

forever bringing things oot.
And puttin it aw back when the faither came in.

Aye, mither?
Aye, faither. She'd say.

But the faither wondered,

What's happened tae they two lassies?
Ach, he thought, with war oan in Glasgow,
there was tae much runnin aroond.

Upstairs, Gallacher and Lizzie were always getting ready to go out some-
where,
filling the room with curlers and clothes and stockings
and when they didn't have real stockings
they drew a line on the backs of their legs with a pencil,

    aye. Jist couldnae wait tae go oot there
    tae see what everyone was wearin and doin, imagine.
    Glasgow people *really* goan oot,
    mixing with others from aw over the world,
    they werenae goan te miss oot.

At the Locarno, the girls stood and watched the Americans,
so relaxed

    wi they long arms swingin an they long legs dancin.
    Tha wan looks like Tyrone Power.
    Over there it's Joel McCrea.

    They'd never seen the likes,
    couldnae believe their eyes.
    Ach, they American soldiers.

One afternoon
Gallacher was sitting on the upstairs balcony at the Locarno
and an American Navy Sea-man came right over and said:

    This chair taken?

Gallacher looked up. Dana Andrews.

    No, go right ahead, said Gallacher.

And after aw the deals she made with God in the Anderson shelter
with the bombs whistling above her head,

God, if ye let me live Ah will...

Ach,

it didnae mean no dancing,
no goan tae the pictures
no speaking tae they poor haimless soldiers when, after aw,

the next day they might be dead.

Ach,

God didnae expect yehs tae stop yer enjoyment ay life.
Ye jist had tae make up yer mind.
As Jesus Ehsel said:
Ye jist have tae keep oan goan.

No, that seat is not taken, Gallacher said.
And the Navy Sea-man
wi tha blue uniform
sat right doon. Turned oot eh was aff the Scots. Turned oot
eh jist came aff a submarine, been doon fer months an ach,
the Locarno was ehs first breath ay fresh air.

Gallacher thought,

He looks a wee bit far away.
Could be America did that tae him,
surrounded wi aw they
know-what-they're-daein types.
Couldnae be easy over there
when yehs were a wee bit sensitive.

He took a deep breath and Gallacher thought,

> Course, could've been tha quiet doon in the water
> even wi U-boats circlin roond.
> Ye'd feel a bit pinned in.
> Ach, they Americans.
> Ye had tae be so certain ay yersel over there.

She glanced over at him.

> Nay room fer a sliver ay doot.

As someone said,

> One thing Ah'll say aboot they Americans,
> they didnae jist talk. Ach.
> They took action.
> Still an aw.

She glanced over. Dana Andrews. Tall.

> Didnae say much. Didnae talk a lot ay nonsense.
> Then eh said eh felt hemmed in under aw tha water. Eh said,
> at times eh couldnae take it, felt like eh'd never get oot.

> Ach, looking oot the windae in Glasgow,
> she understood.

He went on, told her different things, about his family,
Gallacher imagined a house with a mither like her mither,
everything the same

> jist bigger.

Gallacher listened.

He was a fine fella.
Then eh asked,
straight oot:
Would you like to dance?

The way Americans said things,
aw the girls at the table smiled.
After aw they debacles slidin doon bannisters,
the Americans looked like princes, b'jove.

She stood up
to walk down to the dance floor
when the American Navy Sea-man,

ach, Dana Andrews, asks:

Which way are you going down?

It was a funny thing to say.

The stairs, she answered.
And the American Navy Sea-man said,

Ah know a quicker way.

Gallacher walked down the stairs to the dance floor
and on the way down that long winding staircase,
she saw him,
the American Navy Sea-man,
Dana Andrews,

leap right over the railing,
an go straight doon.

The music stopped. They all rushed in.
But he was gone, killed on impact.

Someone said,

> Airmen are like that. It goes fer the head.

An American officer asked Gallacher what the soldier told her
before he leapt and she said,

> Eh jist took a deep breath an went.

The officer took over.
Took away the body of the American Navy Sea-man,
told Gallacher not to tell anyone what he said,
whatever it was, but she thought,

> Eh didnae say a thing. Ach,
> eh jist went.

After, walking down the street,

> suddenly aw they five foot twos and threes
> didnae look so bad.

But ach. They American soldiers.

> It wasnae aw ha ha ha.

After all, there was a war on. Work to go to.
Back in Glasgow, after the mines, the milk delivery,
the ice cream, the pigs, the telegraph poles,
for Gallacher it wasn't all fizzy drinks,
or chimney sweeps, or wood shacks where you could read.
That was all gone with the war. With the war
there was no reading, no devils in cemeteries,
no headless figures on Vimy Ridge,

ach.

After a while ye didnae even have stories.
Jist rations
and goan tae work.

Gallacher took a job at Woolworth's on Union Street in Glasgow.
Gallacher was worried going in

    didnae think she could count
    aw tha confusin money:
    shillings, pence, hapennys, thruppeny bits, ach.

The night before her first day at work
she stared at the ceiling and thought

    Ah cannae

until she just got up the next morning,
went to work and started counting for herself:

    shillings, pence, hapennys, thruppeny bits, ach.

    Nine-day wonder.

Pretty soon she was flying through

    shillings, pence, hapennys, thruppeny bits like winky
    in aw the different departments: china, boot goods, polish and brushes,
    gloves, scarves and handbags, counting
    shillings, pence, hapennys, thruppeny bits, like the toot.

She was in charge of every department she was in.
She liked accessories
and the music in Woolworth's played over the speakers,

Ella and Louis,
shillings, pence, hapennys, thruppeny bits,
ach.

A tisket, a tasket. Tomato-tomahto. It was liberty
even with Mr. O'Byrne the boss starin doon at yehs.
Everyone was afraid of him,
he was so stern, Mr. O'Byrne.

Sitting upstairs in an eight-sided glass booth
where he could see the shop girls weighing and counting

shillings, pence, hapennys and thruppeny bits,
ach.

Miss McGuinty worked beside Gallacher
and she used to start each day saying,

Ah cannae wait tae get oota here.
When Ah get called up fer service Ahm goan,
Ahm tellin yehs.

If you had a job you could get out of munitions duty,
and Gallacher said,

Oh aye, me too. Ahm goan as well.

All the girls said it.
It was the thing to say
and Miss McGuinty just said,

Oh Ah cannae wait.

One day Mr. O'Byrne called Gallacher up to the eight-sided booth.
Miss McGuinty looked up from men's socks,

Wonder what that's aboot.

But Mr. O'Byrne said,

> Miss Toibin, you are very quick with shillings, pence,
> hapennys and thruppeny bits.
> Ach, eh was so stern.
> He had an English accent,
> very correct, aw put together.

He said,

> There is an opening in the candy department.
> I would like you to try it, Miss Toibin.

Biscuits was the busiest.
But it was the best, the most interesting.

> Yes, Mr. O'Byrne, she said
> and went doon the stairs

while Miss McGuinty stared.

Her first day was a Saturday
and Saturdays in Glasgow everyone lined up for sweets,
it was the day for it,
and the line up at the long counter went twice around,

> aw they mithers, the mither included,

Mr. O'Byrne keeping a close eye

> tae see if Gallacher was fast enough
> weighing oot the biscuits and sweets
> aw they different kinds

and she flew through

shillings, pence, hapennys and thruppeny bits

but Mr. O'Byrne couldnae believe it,

She is quick. But is she accurate?

He asked Gallacher's supervisor, Ms. McGonigal,
from the eight-sided glass room.

Ms. McGonigal, would you please go down and see
if Ms. Toibin's scales are accurate.

And Ms. McGonigal went downstairs
and the mither heard her say,

Tha one's quick.

And someone else said,

An she's accurate.

Every time Gallacher weighed cookies she was right on the mark.
And in two years, at eighteen, Gallacher was made a supervisor.
She wore a blue uniform with the word *Supervisor* on the front,
she looked so young, when the American soldiers came in,
she heard one say to the other,

The foreman went to France,
jist like ye'd hear in the pictures.

Ach, aw the kids were in charge.

But Gallacher had a mind of her own
and one day Mr. O'Byrne said,

Miss Toibin I would like you to display the hand fashions
over here. Please bring the display with you.

But Gallacher thought,

A way over there doesnae make sense.

And Mr. O'Byrne said,

Miss Toibin I have a very busy schedule this morning,
please come this way.

But Gallacher said,

No, Ahm sorry Mr. O'Byrne.
Ah cannae display the gloves over there.

Mr. O'Byrne stood up straight.

Miss Toibin, come this way. And bring the display.

Gallacher said,

Ah cannae dae it Mr, O'Byrne. It doesnae make sense.
I think the gloves should be here in the accessories,
with the rest. The gloves belong doon here, Mr. O'Byrne.
Ach.

By this time all the girls had gathered around,
including Miss McGuinty.
Mr. O'Byrne stared straight intae Gallacher's eyes
and Gallacher stared straight back.

That'll be all Miss Toibin, said Mr. O'Byrne.

Miss McGuinty, bring the hand fashion display over here,

and Miss McGuinty ran right over.

And Gallacher went straight home.

Ahm no goan back, she told the mither.
Mr. O'Byrne an tha Miss McGuinty.

The mither wrang her hands.
Lassie!

Mum, Ah wiz right an eh knew it.
An oh, eh wiz mad.
Ah cannae go back.

Aye,
Lassie, it's awright.
Ah know how much yeh love the job noo.

But Gallacher said,

Ahm no goan.

And the mither took aff her apron,
threw on her coat
went doon Union Street on the tram car,
walked through the doors of Woolworths

with that hard step

walked right up tae Mr. O'Byrne's office
an whatever the mither said,
she didnae say,
but the mither said Mr. O'Byrne liked Gallacher

and he told the mither,

> You tell Miss Toibin to report here for work
> tomorrow morning at 9 o'clock.

After that they got along great.
But then Miss McGuinty started telling everyone
about Mr. O'Byrne,

> the girls talked, aye.

> It aw gets oot in the department stores.
> Ye'd never know it tae look at ehm but

his wife was English, wore a slim pink suit, a real lady buddy.

> They had two children, and ach,
> she left him fer an English soldier named Moore.
> Imagine.

Someone said,

> Poor Mr. O'Byrne. Tha Irish bit. Didnae see it comin.

> Ach.
> Shillings, pence, hapennys, thruppeny bits,
> ye could always count oan *it*.

Gallacher and Lizzie were both called up to work
in the munitions factory
and Miss McGuinty said,

> Ach. Ah envy yoos.
> When my time comes up Ahm goan too.
> Cannae wait.

Lizzie went over the border to Birmingham.
She boarded with a woman with two small children,
husband fighting overseas. It was the times.

Lizzie didnae know what wiz goan oan under tha roof,
but at breakfast each morning there wiz always
a new British soldier sittin there eatin his eggs, ever so polite.
Everyone smiling away.

Lizzie aye figured oot
eh wiznae sleepin oan the couch
cuz that's where Lizzie wiz aye sleeping.

She wiz a good woman. It wiz the war.

The British army wasnae looking after her,
an she needed money.
She wiz jist takin care ay her children.

For Gallacher, there were no fizzy drinks
with green bubbles this time,
no reading in the dim light of the chimney sweep's.

Ach. No satin pillas.

Gallacher now went to work.
Evening shift.
Twelve-hours shifts in a grey uniform and hairnet.
It was a Rolls Royce factory converted into a plant
for making airplane parts and she stood on an assembly line where

everyone had a part. Ye picked it up when it passed
and ye added somethin tae it: a ring er a hook.

Yehs never got te see what ye were makin in the end.

Ye just passed it tae the next girl, waited fer yers tae come along,
then passed it tae the next.

Gallacher loved her part.
She thought it looked like a diamond.

But twelve-hour shifts, one and a half hours each way by bus,
two bus changes. It was in Hillington near Paisley.

This wasnae the ding ay the streetcar,
goan tae work jist doon the road;
it wasnae the milk truck er kids and marbles
even in the rain an cold.

It wasnae cousins
Richard Nixon oan a bicycle
er Johnny Lennon waving to yehs
er Tammy standin in an apron waitin oan pigs.

Jist workin wi machines. This wiz war

and everything slipped, the rules were different

faces torn aff
hair caught in machines,
aw they near misses
an hits
made yer head spin.

One evening she waited for the bus but it never stopped.
She had to run, she missed the door
and was dragged across the street before the bus finally stopped.
With bloody knees she made it to work and her boss said,

What kept you late?

Talk aboot the Nazis.
This wiz war.
The kinds ay jobs
that make ye sick.
Jobs that kill yehs.

(Tom Dick and Harry, said the faither.
Makes yeh think.)

Gallacher had boils on her skin
and her face turned pale.
She had to get a special dispensation from the doctor to quit.

An when she went back tae Woolworths, ach.
Miss McGuinty wiz still there,
in Gallacher's supervisor job.

She wiz called up
but turns oot
she turned it doon.

And Miss McGuinty said,

Yeh have tae be kidding. Give up aw this?

It wasnae aw ha ha ha. No.
There was a war oan.

And what did Jesus Ehsel say?
Trust no man.

✳

During the war Tom had one love but it didn't last.
Never mind the heart murmur or sweeping floors

at Dennison Palais, never mind the tea tray he carried
across a mine field. For Tom the war held no romance.

An in Glasgow
if yeh were short
ye knew it.
In fact, they reminded you.
They sang songs at school, in the street,
at work, in the shops,

shorty-yew, shorty-yew,

they reminded you and reminded you,
reminded you and reminded you until

yer shoulders sloped lower an lower
makin ye shorter an shorter
til they'd have a new song:

bull shoulders, bull shoulders.

An the more ye slumped,
the more songs they had tae sing.
Ach aye, in Glasgow, wee was big.

But, so was tall.

They had songs fer tall fellas too.
Tall fellas, head in the clouds.
They didnae trust yehs if ye wiz too far aff the ground.

An there's words over there
that'll cut yeh to a T;
always pointin oot people walkin doon the street.

So cheeky.
And if yeh got mad, kicked a can,
hurt yer foot, there'd be throngs ay kids after ye,

singing

    Limpy Dan, Limpy Dan,
    daa dee dee, an away he ran.

So when the war started,

    wi aw they soldiers wanderin roond
    it wasnae a good time to be wee.

For Tom, chances were limited as it was.
He worked in the munitions steel works in Glasgow.
He went to work, came home,
played football on a team of Protestants,

    ach. They aw loved Tom an life wiz good
    as long as he didnae have tae walk intae a dancehall,
    er worse, speak.

Over there,

    ye jist accepted it.
    Ye made the best ay it.

He was a Rodgers, he would last.
The mither's faither was so good natured, so calm.
The Rodgers were so holy,

    Sam Rodgers prayed aw the time.
    Once he prayed oan ehs knees so long
    he had tae be lifted intae bed in the praying position
    an sleep aw night wi ehs knees bent.

Oot like winky.
So good natured, he slept the whole night.

And Tom was like the mither and the mither's faither,

he didnae mind
carrying trays oot an in
then sittin doon on the oldest chair.

Ach, a pleasant fella.

Someone was always saying,

Tam, ye'll meet somewan.
Just yew wait.
Even if ye never go oot.

But as soon as he'd leave the room,
someone would say,

Sometimes people donnae meet anyone, tha's true.
Aye.

And someone else said,

Still an aw, sometimes yer better aff
wi nowan.

But then, he met *Mary Flynn.*
No one was sure where they met,

ye couldnae get a thing oota him.
They went oan wan date

then

two dates,

and Tom started to think,

This might be it, the wan fer me.

And he started to tell her things, like,

Ah'd like tae make this a wee bit more permanent,

and she'd say,

Oh, aye.

Then one day she said,

Ah like yeh Tam. Ah really do. But

yer
just
tae
quiet.

Tae quiet? thought Tom.

Fer days he didnae say a word
an all he could hear in his own head was:

QUIET.

The word was in his head for weeks
like a heart beat,

quiet. QUIET.
Quiet. QUIET.

An it wasnae a murmur this time, no,
but a shout, loud and clear.

He thought,

If a lassie needs a lot ay fly chat,
then Ah have tae be practical.
Ah donnae have any fly chat.

He had luck, that Rodgers bit.
He wiz calm, could tell a joke.
But if the lassies liked fly chat,
it wouldnae work, an ach,
maybe it wiz a relief.

So after tha, he didnae bother.
After tha, he jist stayed home,
carried in the tray,
sat in the chair.
Listened to his heart beat.

※

The war dragged oan. It jist wasnae the same.
But there wiz no feelin sorry fer yersehl over there.
An there was always someone tae remind yehs
tae no take yersehl tae seriously.

After aw, self-pity was jist the devil.
An in Scotland,
the devil was big.

Omnipresent, the priest said,
(when he wasnae running aboot Vimy Ridge). Ach.

Ye didnae ask questions.
And if yeh jist kept oan goan
he stayed oot the way.

Aye, ye just kept goan.
Keep right oan til the end ay the road.

When Gallacher's little brother Sam, three years old,
died of whooping cough, he lay in state for three days.
Gallacher visited him by his bed

    wi his wee night goon oan, aw white.
    After they took Sam away
    the mither didnae touch the bed
    er the dent oan the pilla,
    waited til the air naturally went oot, ach.
    Ye jist accepted it. Ye kept goan.

Losing Willie, last month of the war, shot in the back, devil er no,
ach. Sometimes aw life seemed tae produce
wiz sadness,
but yehs accepted it.

Yehs had tae.
Yehs had tae remember cousin John,
the mither's brother's James Faulkner's son,
the wan left alone when the family went oan holidays. Ach.
They returned to find him aw peely wally
listening tae a record ay Gregorian chant
over and over, night and day, oan and oan,
they wondered what happened tae him.

Someone said,

    Aw tha education – went fer ehs napper.
    Philosophy. Theology. Ach. It went oan fer weeks:

lyin in bed, listenin tae Gregorian chant,
until ehs faither said,
What's the matter wi him? What's aye up?

Eh cannae work, his maw said, bringin in the tray.
Cannae work? Ehs faither said.
Ach, sore this, sore tha.

Trays in an oot aw day.
Mither? He'd call doon.
Where's ma chips?
Gregorian chant goan like the toot upstairs

and someone said

Do ye think ehs aye pushin it a wee bit tae far noo?

Mither bringin trays up and doon, ehs poor mither.
Jist like the mither an aw they other mithers wi tha hard step
runnin after aw they wains
up and doon the stairs
even wi the wains, ach,
turnin middle aged.
Aw day tha record goan, chantin,
Kyrie oan an oan,
big licks
until it started tae go fer the faither's napper.

The men gathered.

They said,

Poor John er no, this cannae continue.
Aye, eh's driving us aw nuts.

It's no way tae live.

Mither, they said.
We're goan in there tae pull ehm oot.

And the mither said,

Ach, no. Eh cannae go. Ahm telling ye. Ehs tha weak.

So aw the men went up
an burst intae John's room
an unplugged the record player.

Yer goan tae get a job, said the men, ripping aff the sheets.

Nae more wee trays ay sweets, ach.
Aye, an nae more ay they jam rolls.

Aye! It's they jam rolls!
No! It wiz the record player!
Tha Gregorian chant. Aye! Look!

They sat ehm up in the chair.
John blinked like tha wee newborn pig,
jist the wan,
and he agreed. Aye,
eh took it a wee bit too far.
Ah didnae know what happened.

Thanks fellas,
was aw he said.

An the next day John put oan a nice jacket
went oot
an found a job.
That was the end ay it.

It didnae take much. As someone said,
Aw he needed was tae get oota bed.

So Gallacher went back to work at her job at Woolworth's,
in gloves, was made a supervisor again, back counting

shillings, pence, hapennys, thruppeny bits, ach.

Best thing she ever did.

VI

Pas de Basque to 2B with RF (count '1' and '2');
assemble at 2 with RF in front (count '3');
disassemble, taking RF to Third Rear Aerial Position.

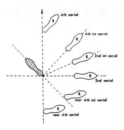

And then,
one day in Woolworth's Department Store
on Sauchiehall Street,

    Nelson Eddy walked oot ay the trees.

He was with five other Canadian soldiers
dressed in moss green
and one of them said to Lizzie,

    What does a fella do here in the evening for entertainment?

All the girls turned.

    Ach. They Canadians had a fly chat aw their own.

Lizzie said,

    My sister works in the Woolworth's on Union Street.
    Maybe she'd like tae go dancin
    er tae the pictures.

The next day, a Canadian came in to Woolworth's
and asked for Gallacher but Gallacher

aye had her *lady friend* visitin
and she wiz lyin a way doon in a back room upstairs.
Everday Gallacher did her best,
tried tae look neat, but this wasnae the day,
ach, no wi her lady friend visitin.

One of the girls burst in,

Gallacher, there's a Canadian here tae see yehs
an yehs have tae come doon right noo.
Ye jist have tae come doon right noo an see this fella!
But Gallacher couldnae, it was tha bad.

Tell ehm no. Tell ehm tae come back another day.

And the next day, he never came.
The next day, the same.
Three days later, well.
The next day was a Wednesday, a slow day.
She was standing outside the counter,
tidying away,
when she heard a voice behind her say,

Are you Miss Toibin?

In that cheerful voice.

Ach, it sounded jist like the ootdoors.
Like Nelson Eddy callin straight through they evergreens
an when she turned aroond, standin there
was this Canadian soldier:

so pleasant, nice smile, so clean, he said,

Your sister said to come over.

Gallacher stood.

Oh?

Would you like to go to a movie? he asked.

Simple as that, no footerin aboot.
No philosophy aboot lassies an gettin tied doon.
No keekin roond corners tae see if anyone wiz lookin,
even aw though the other shopgirls
were aw keekin oot.
Even Mr. O'Byrne must have got an eyeful from a way up there.

Oh yes, said Gallacher,

aw professional shopgirl, no playin games.

That would be nice, she said.

They went out for dinner on the Friday,
then they started writing back and forth.
He was different from the rest.

No satin pillas, no fly chat.
No leapin doon balconies. Ach.
Jist Nelson Eddy with tha hair, they manners,
tha clear voice and
a nicely shaped head.

He went to the front
then came back four months later for one week,

then he went to Italy. There were letters and letters.
Then she never heard for a long time.

    Aye, Gallacher still went oot wi other fellas, after aw
    she wasnae tied doon yet. She still went tae the Locarno
    and the dances.

    But things were gettin desperate fer the local men;
    hard tae compete wi aw they men at the front
    writin love letters tae the lassies.

Turns out Nelson Eddy was injured at Monte Cassino,
shrapnel in the leg, he went to hospital, wasn't allowed to write.
Three months went by and one day,
Gallacher came home from work and saw a letter waiting.
The mither's eyes lit up.

    Ach.

There was something different about Nelson Eddy,

    in they eyes,
    in tha face,
    there was no comparin
    him wi other fellas because,

as someone said,

    ye jist couldnae compare.
    Nelson was aye in a class ay ehs own.

When he returned from Italy with the injury he came to visit
and Gallacher was nervous to see him. She wondered
if she'd feel the same. They'd gotten closer on paper but

yeh never know.

It was a Thursday and the first thing Gallacher noticed,

> Nelson Eddy grew two inches taller in Italy.
> It's true, eh said. It was the bread.
> No like in Canada, where he almost starved tae death.

He stayed at the house ten days. They went for walks,
talked with the mither and even the faither knew

> he couldnae stop Nelson Eddy
> walkin oota they evergreens
> like a mountie on a horse. Ye jist couldnae.

The faither liked him.
In fact the faither walked into the living room
when he saw Nelson
and said,

> Oh aye, take a seat,

and everyone's eyes flew open
they'd never heard such a thing from the faither.

And when they took Nelson Eddy to the parish church
Nelson said he liked it there,
he was the tallest one
and he could see the altar for a change.

> Ach. The way Nelson said things, aw serious.

The mither said,

> When Nelson walked intae a room, he lit it up.
> Somethin aboot him.

Yehs jist couldnae wait tae see ehm
er wait tae hear
what eh'd say next.

One day they were out for a walk
and Nelson Eddy looked a wee bit nervous.
It was a Monday and Nelson Eddy said,

Let's go to Edinburgh.

They took the train
and it was about 9 o'clock
and the stores were open.

Ach. Nelson had somethin planned, she jist knew.
Yeh could see the wee wheels workin.

He took Gallacher's arm into a jeweller,

she still wasnae thinking aboot anythin specific
an he led her up tae the counter an said tae the fella,

Ah'd like to see some rings.

And Gallacher thought,

Well, maybe eh'd like tae buy a dress ring fer ehself.
A *man's ring*, as they said in America.

An oot comes the tray.

Oh, aye, the shop clerk says, very willing.

And Nelson Eddy says to Gallacher in that clear voice,

Which one do you like?

Even the fella looked at ehm.

Gallacher says,

> Well, Ah kinda knew it was comin
> wi aw they letters.
> Ah didnae have tae think aboot it long.
>
> Ah picked oot a wee wan
> with a wee daisy shaped stone
> and eh put it oan mah finger.

It was March 26th, 1945 and they walked up to the castle.
It was freezing.

> A fella was blowin the pipes:
> *Lament for a Dead Soldier.*

When they got back to Glasgow, Lizzie opened the door
and Gallacher put out her hand, and oh, she was happy for them.

> Gallacher's engaged!

And they were aw huggin each other an it was a fine day
an the mither an even the faither said,

> Nelson, yer a fine man.

Word spread. Ach.
As soon as Willie O'Leary's mither heard the news,
she didnae speak to the mither at church for six months
an one day she finally spoke.

She just glared,

> Well. What wiz wrang wi oor Willie?

Ach. Willie hadnae even said hello!

And someone said,

Yer the first wan te marry a foreigner.

But the war.
March 26th, 1945.
It took five days for the telegram to arrive.
Willie was killed that day.

The mither said,
God took Wullie.
And sent Nelson Eddy.

※

The war ended in June and they all moved to London
where there were weddings every day
but Gallacher couldn't find a dress.

Nelson Eddy, eh was so kind, so Canadian, ach.
They think ay everything.
Eh ordered wan from Canada:
heavy satin princess type.
Lily point sleeve. Satin buttons. Plain collar.

And it arrived
the day they left for their honeymoon
in Blackpool.

So instead she wore pale blue.
That day at Church of the Sacred Heart, London,
down by Victoria Station, with her hair full of curls,
she wore a great big hat,

ach.
Looked like she could fly away in it.

The faither was the best dressed in striped trousers
and two-tone shoes. At the Dorchester Hotel,
when the fella who leads the lobby orchestra
saw the couple coming through the revolving doors,

    Nelson in tha moss green uniform,
    Gallacher in pale blue and a big hat,

he struck up the band
and she forgot what they played but ach,

    she never fergot
    swingin through they doors
    wi Nelson Eddy,
    an the music playin.

After Blackpool
after the wedding
after the war

Nelson Eddy was stuck in barracks for two months
polishing brass, waiting to be de-mobbed,
while Gallacher worked in London in Woolworth's again,

    back tae
    shillings, pence, hapennys, thruppeny bits

while in her mind it

    was aw Nelson Eddy and Jeannette MacDonald
    singin in the trees, ach.

Shillings, pence, hapennys, thruppeny bits,
aw the while she counted at the till
she couldnae get her mind aff

pictures of Canada she'd seen in school books:

campfires,

Ten and six
mountains, ach, the Rockies,
Three and five

prairies in summer,

splittin stones,
Four and eight

and someone said,

Trees grow tall where the people grow tall—
ye jist had te be born in the right place.

But Gallacher worried.

They Canadian women knew how tae cook
knew how tae can and pickle and bake, ach.
Eight and ten.
Aw they pies and roasts, ach, even antelope.

Two oceans.
Five and nine.
Ach, a bargain.

December 1945, Christmas Day.
Nelson left for Canada
to make the way.

✳

Gallacher couldnae wait tae leave
even aw though

she'd miss the ones back home, the ones who'd stay.

She'd miss Loudie, a nun,
and Loudie's mither, Mary,
and her faither Hugh and brother Sam, a teacher,
who'd become a headmaster in Glasgow
who ended up almost blind, he wore glasses so thick

    ye could barely see him.
    Poor Sam, eh could barely make yehs oot,
    tha blind, but he knew yeh by yer voice.

Gallacher was going to miss the old country,
people you liked to be around,
even older Tommy and Dick rocking by the fire

    who'd aye be doing nothin aw day from noo on
    but talkin aboot her in Canada.

She could hear them,

    After aw, leavin Scotland
    an goan tae Canada, aye Dick?
    Aye, Canada isnae America. Isnae New York, Tammy.
    It's a totally different thing.
    Even aw though, Tammy.
    Aye, Dick, even aw though.

She'd miss them.

May, Loudie's sister, was adopted,
she liked to be in charge,
wore thick black stockings in all weather,

black dress, a woman who'd laugh when it was funny

but wouldnae otherwise.

May, so steady, a woman who'd look after you when you were sick.
And Hugh, a ship's captain who married a teacher
who became a headmistress in England, Anne.
And Sam, another brother, another teacher
who became another headmaster
in another school in Glasgow.

And Mary, May's sister, a teacher,
who would die of pneumonia at twenty-eight.

And James, another brother,
who worked in a factory
who married a teacher, Rosemary,
who was Gallacher's teacher,

who had another sister
who was another teacher
who became a headmistress
at another school in Glasgow
who married
another
teacher.

And another cousin, Mary,

the wan wi tha nice roond face,
black hair, quiet, she died of old age.

Ye know how people seem to just die over there,
fer no reason.

And Agnes, a teacher

oh yes, who never married, who lived with her sister, Nellie,
a secretary, up at the top of Quarrybrae Street in that sitting room
with linen doilies and green mementos of Carfin Grotto.

Agnes and Nellie were Gallacher's favourites,
they used to give Gallacher their old clothes,

so lovely and neat, suits and dresses,
always wi gloves an shoes an scarves to go wi it,
good cloth, so lovely, every year
they'd bring oot their old clothes
so Gallacher and Lizzie could pick.

Agnes, who always had watery eyes from the Glasgow wind;
she who loved kids, was kind, she told stories with Nellie
with good punch lines, Agnes and Nellie, ach,

talk about Tom, Dick and Harry, they could tell yehs
aw the ways people died over there,
and it wisnae jist pneumonia.

Over the years Agnes and Nellie watched them all go:

Cathy, a teacher with a great sense of humour
with cats-eye glasses,
the aunt who understood everything,
who sent Jimmy down the road
for frozen fish sticks
when the Canadian visitors arrived.

Oh Cathy,

who didnae care aboot bakin pies, pickling or canning
er any ay tha. An ach. They Brogans could dress.
Pink boucle two-piece with a belted vest.
Green slippers with satin trim thread.
Black and cream dress shoes wi long laces.

Cathy was the aunt
who'd kneel by yer side
tae show ye pictures
of Blackpool's famous rides.

Oh, Cathy.
From another time.

How she went in the end.
Electrocuted by a towel warmer.

Ach. Glasgow.
Ye survived teachers wi rulers
factory machines
bombs in shelters
quilts in trees

bad jobs, bad bosses, bad pay, bad food, bad shoes,

and aw the wee disappointments in between,

then ye took a bath, an ach.
Bad plumbing.

So when someone said,

Look at Tom, Dick an Harry.
Better tae stay poot.

Someone else said,

Ehs no aboot stayin poot. Ach.
Get that intae yer head.

Nelson arrived in Canada:
January 1, 1946.

※

But, ach. The ways people died over there.

Granny Toibin's (Annie McDermid Rodgers') faither, Sam Rodgers,
was a saint. He was once ambushed by highway robbers.
Sam used to put raw eggs in his coat pocket and when he cracked them
by mistake, he would say,

Daveration character.
Ach, his strongest words.

He married Agnes McNamara,

who didnae die
but they say wiz, ach. Buried alive.
Ask Granny McNamee,
who touched Agnes McNamara's forehead
an found it still warm after five days.

Ach, yehs jist didnae gae intae it.

Some people wanted tae open coffins years later
only to find their relatives
had turned. Yehs jist didnae go intae it.
(Still an aw.)

Between fourteen children,
where seven died and seven lived
with TB, pneumonia, twins (one died),
teachers, headmasters,

      ach. Between Tom Dick and Harry hangin over yer heads,
      even aw though ye wanted tae leave,
      it was hard te make a move.

She'd miss them.

Agnes's daughter Agnes
who married Jim, who had John, Jim,
Sam, Mamie, Nessie, Lizzie and Loudie.

And another Nessie,
who had a straight back,
a teacher people loved,
who was fun at parties
but who could just turn;
she married Charlie McCullough,
a headmaster with a thin moustache

      who wasnae tall
      but could tell a joke.

She had one daughter
who became a nun
who was sent to England;
she could only visit once every six years.

And once,
on her six-year visit,
she went to open her mother's door,

but she couldnae open it,
because Nessie was lyin oan the floor, ach.
Charlie long dead.
Nessie had been gone five days before anywan found her
in the middle of a heat wave.

Ach.
Yeh jist didnae go intae it.

※

There was always Patrick Lennon tae consider.

A good man, son of Lizzie. Patrick,
the perfect height, he wore pin stripes, smoked pipes

with tha lovely Toibin hair.
He had a nice gait, good posture.

He owned a shoe store in downtown Glasgow.
He had even white teeth.
He ran a good business, taking care

of aw they bunions an corns ay Glasgow women
in their Kitty Kelly cardboard shoes
tha melted in the rain.

He used to say,

Ah never found a foot Ah couldnae find a shoe fer
and his motto was: *Give me yer worst feet.*

Every year he took his family to Ireland on holiday.
Always Ireland,

aw though, the mither said.

We're Scottish noo, a few generations in.

But that didnae mean a thing to aw they
Toibins, Lennons, Rodgers, McDermids,
Gallachers, McNamaras and McNamees.

And everyone knew, years ago, the first Toibin was French.
Captain Tobere fought in the war in Ireland
and fell in love with an Irish girl
who said she'd never leave home soil.
So he moved to Ireland instead,
even changed his name to Toibin,
someone said,

    Ach, no.
    Use yer napper!
    Toibins were Irish
    to begin wi.

Someone else said the Toibins left Ireland
when a stable boy fell in love with a Toibin,
a wealthy landowner's daughter
and they ran away,

    eloped to Scotland, ach.
    That wiz love.

As Patrick Lennon used to say,

    We're aw Irish over here anyway.

And that year, as usual,
Patrick closed the shop for the holiday.

It was 1963.
Patrick returned from his annual trip,

walked through the door,
his face all lit up,
and in a big loud voice, he said:

See Ireland and die!

And he dropped dead.

Jist like that. Ask Tom.
Ach. Aye.

There was always Patrick Lennon tae consider.

※

July 1946, Gallacher left Southampton.
Getting ready to leave,
five days by ship, four by train,
thinking about Nelson Eddy
singing in the trees,

Oh Rose Marie,
Ah hmm mmm.

Nine days by ship, four by train was all she could think
until she walked down the dock
and turned to the mither beside her

weepin intae tha hanky, dabbin her eyes, ach,
always seein children aff at trains
an boats wi tha hanky, sayin,
We might no ever see yehs again.

And the faither saying,

Aye, Nelson Eddy, we hardly know the fella.

The whole family was out to see Gallacher off.
They hurried down the dock and saw a tall stately ship,
big as the Queen Mary and Gallacher thought,

Oh, five days oan tha ship!

And the faither said,

Ach, they'll probably gie yehs a good cabin
jist fer marryin a Canadian soldier and aw

and they all laughed, when

Tam, who always seemed tae notice
what was goan oan, said:
That's no the ship.

With a cigarette in his hand
he pointed to the ship beside it,

Aye. This wan's yoors over here.

Ach. The Lady Nelson.
A banana boat from Panama.
Leanin oan the dock wi a short stack.

Aye, the jokes were flying.
Ehs no the Titanic, quipped Tam.
No, said the faither, yeh wullnae die of luxury.

And someone said,

Wan thing Ah'll say aboot they wee ships,
they're strong. Made fer the waves.
An they get yehs through.
Even aw though.

It was time.
Tom moved up and gave Gallacher's shoulder a hug.

She couldnae believe it, in public an aw.
Tam had aye changed since the days ay Dennison Palais,
since the minefield, the heart murmur,
since Mary Flynn.

Ach.

Gallacher knew the world was changing.
And the faither told her to be safe and said,

Ach, five days by ship, four by train, like a holiday.
Donnae look back lassie, he said.
An donnae compare yersehl tae others.
Tell yersehl yer nae better
an no worse
than anywan else.

Gallacher thought,

Ah'll remember tha,
wi aw they Canadian lassies skinnin rabbits
an antelope.

The faither said goodbye.
There were hugs
and the mither was crying and dabbing her eyes

wi tha hanky
wi the faither tellin her,
Jist mind, noo mither, jist mind.
Donnae make it harder noo.

Ach, after aw, the faither aye understood,
he'd been te war.

Even aw though.

The thought that Gallacher might never see the mither again
with they big comfortable arms,

walkin doon the street
arm in arm, best friends, ach.
Tae say goodbye tae yer own maither – forever.

Walking up the ship's plank alone
with that straight back,
her curls and big brown hat,
was the first time
her feet had been off home soil

and she felt dizzy,
a little bit sick,

but with that straight back,
and the Rodgers dark curls,
and those blue eyes,
she kept moving forward.

The mither's hanky waving
like she was already gone.

Not even oot the harbour,
the city movin farther and farther away,
that ship goan up and doon,

she stood on the deck looking at the warehouses and brick buildings,
she'd never seen her family or home from so far away before,

farther and farther an away they went.

Someone on deck said,

> A haime's a haime fer aw tha.

> Gallacher knew the mither wiz oot there
> somewhere,
> dabbin her eyes wi tha hanky.

And later, someone said,

> The mither wiz the last wan tae leave. Ach,
> she waited til the ship was well oota sight,
> like it was a train,
> wavin up at the windaes,
> like she could still see yehs.

Tom, with his hands in his pockets, said,

> She's away.

And remembered Willie.

> *Tom. Ahm never coming back again.*

Gallacher wasn't homesick for long.

> She didnae know
> tha leavin the ground,
> aw that up and doon
> could make yeh sick
> an not even oot the harbour,
> mither's hankie still wavin,

Gallacher went below, seasick for three days.

Ach.

Five days by ship, she got to know the waves,
every plunge and dip,
every side to side,
every churn and twist
like it was a dance step.
So sick, so sick.
And the whole ship knew.
A Canadian nurse wrote a poem about it
for the ship's newsletter, about the Scottish girl who was seasick,

The sounds re-echoing aff the walls,

but finally, three days into the five,
Gallacher walked up the stairs
from below, past artillery, infantry and foot soldiers,
and she never felt better.
The sea got rougher and rougher
but she was over it.

It was a medical ship and all the injured soldiers
on deck knew her and smiled,

Poor kid.
Ach. The way they say things.
She wanted tae tell Lizzie,
wished she was right there.

She never felt stronger in her life,
wi tha fresh breeze an everywan lookin oot fer her.
The Atlantic wiz calm the rest ay the way.

She shared a room with a Welsh girl with a six-month-old baby
who'd married a Canadian from the prairies.

Right in the middle ay the middle ay nowhere, she said.
But oh, she couldnae wait to see him. He was a fine man.

Ach, they agreed. They Canadian soldiers.

There was a girl on the ship named Mary,

a naïve lassie,
a brand new bride

on her way to Canada,
first time out of England.

Caught oan an upper deck where the officers met.
She wasnae supposed tae be there
but in aw the excitement, she jist went,
and an officer offered tae light her cigarette,
an he leaned over fer a kiss

jist a kiss, she couldnae resist,
and suddenly

a light shone oan them
and she was caught.
The officer was aff like the toot,

leaving Mary, red faced, a cigarette between her lips.
The army police came along,
brought her down the stairs,

past the men: artillery, infantry and gunners,

and locked her up below.
All the girls were talking about it.
You could hear her crying from the depths.

Ach, Mary.
First time away from home.

In Halifax, husbands lined the shore.
Alone no more.

The war brides saw the men and called oot:
Look, there's meh Johnny, meh Jimmy, meh Stu!
An the men gave a big whoop.
Yeh couldnae hold them back, ach.
They wiz like a herd ay animals
an the girls ran doon the plank,
aw the noise:

Ach, come away wi yeh!

Aw they fellas shoutin:

Sugar! Sweetheart! My girl!
After aw tha distance.

But when Mary started to run with the others
she was stopped halfway,
caught by her wrists.
The headlines said,

Caught fraternizing with an officer of the Canadian army.
Warbride sent back home.

An her husband jist stood,

alone, ach. Waitin oan ehs kiss.

When the Lady Nelson turned around,
Mary went with it.

VII

Execute four High Cuts at 2,
springing RF, LF, RF, LF
(count 1& 2& 3& 4&).

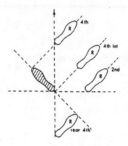

Across Canada the train flew. Brides left the train by the hundreds,
across Manitoba, across Saskatchewan the train flew
and the nearer they got, the nearer and nearer

    five days by ship, four by train,

then only three, then only two,
the stories all got told and the worried ones wondered
if there'd be a husband waiting for them
and the Welsh woman with the baby

    couldnae wait to see hers,

a handsome Canadian. Oh, Gallacher loved the stories,
saw Nelson Eddy at every turn,
at every stop, in every moss green uniform
she saw that forehead. Going home
to someone like Nelson she knew

    she didnae have tae worry.

Before she left home, the mither told her one afternoon
she saw Nelson on the couch, one of the few times
he looked relaxed and the mither said,

Nelson, a penny fer yer thoughts.

And he said,

Ah'm wonderin how Ah'm goan tae find a job.

After that, the mither and the faither didnae worry.
Ach.
Canadians.

The train flew, crossed the prairies, brides left by the hundreds
then by the tens, then by the fives,
and to pass time, Gallacher started counting

shillings, pence, hapennys, thruppeny bits, ach,

until it was down to just a few, to the ones and twos.

But, Ach. Canada. She couldnae believe her eyes.

Lakes and rivers, even better than the movies,

cause when ye walked oot the theatre in Glasgow
yeh were right back intae aw tha soot.
But, Ach. Canada. A country yeh could count oan.

And just like the schoolbook,
outside the window at sundown she saw
smoke drift up from a campfire,

Ten and six
snow on the mountain,

Three and five
big trucks on flat roads,

Four and eight
and someone said,

There's nothin oot there.

Gallacher counted, remembered what the schoolbook said:

Canada produced one fifth of the world's wheat.

Looking out the window she thought,

A man from here had tae be good.
She peered intae the dark
an remembered the mither telling:

Sister Anne, sister Anne is there anybody coming?
No. Nothing but the wind and the green grass blowing.
Sister Anne, sister Anne is there anybody coming?
No. Nothing but the wind and the green grass blowing.
Sister Anne, sister Anne is there anybody coming?
Yes! Bluebeard an he's comin' up the stairs!

Was Bluebeard oot there?

On the train, the two girls were the only ones left.

She was sad tae leave but, Ach,
Canada. Jist look.

Canadian Pacific Railway through the wilderness,
coyotes howling, for once
everything as you thought it would be.

The girls held hands. The baby cried.
There was nothing for miles around and the train came to a halt.
It was the Welsh girl's stop and the conductor came forward,

 It's time to leave.

The girls hugged.
A handsome Canadian soldier would be waiting.

On the prairie in summer, midnight,
the sky wild with stars, a whistling wind
that drew your breath, that changed how you spoke,

 ach.

And outside, no one was
waiting, no soldier, no man, no one.
She went out. The wind whistled
under the baby's blanket

and she cried. Gallacher looked out,

 she couldnae see a thing,

all she could hear was the Welsh lassie crying
in the middle of nowhere.

Gallacher said,

 We have tae bring her in,
 we have tae wait fer her.

The wind whipped.
The conductor said,

We have to keep time.
We can't just sit here on the track with something coming.

He took out his watch. *See?*
Gallacher went outside and stood beside her.

The girl was rooted to the spot.

The conductor came out,

Miss, get back inside.

The Welsh woman stared
up and down, no one.
No soldier, no man, no one,

and someone said,
Ach. Canada.

Gallacher and the Welsh woman and the baby were all crying now,

and tha bloomin wind never let up,

even the conductor had a tear
but he took Gallacher inside
started the train

and left her an tha baby
standin there.

The train gathered steam, headed West. Only one left.

Ach. Canada.

That dark, that wind.

Crossing the prairie

    in space
    so quiet

Gallacher thinking,

    shillings, pence, hapennys, thruppeny bits, ach.

Canada. In the middle of nowhere,
all she could do was count.

EPILOGUE

She finishes her story at a quarter to three.
Her grandparents all died within six months of each other.
She remembers the mither's mither lying on her deathbed,

> lovely woman, snowy white hair, brown eyes,
> lookin at her and Lizzie in their Easter bonnets with big bows.

She said to Gallacher,

> Yer named after me, an mind
> it's Gallacher with a 'ch,' not a 'g' ,
> an it's Rodgers with a 'd,' not a 'g'.

Important in a sea of Toms, Dicks, Harrys, Nellies, Nessies,
Lizzies, Cathys and Sams.
And the faither and mither,
        ach,
followed Gallacher to Canada just a few years later.

And the faither.
One day the mither brought in dessert
and he said:

> Ah'll save tha fer later.

He put his teeth on the bedside tray
and went to sleep.

The mither went to the kitchen, lit the blue flame
for tea and thought,

> Ah didnae like the sound ay tha.
> So she went in.

He'd jist slumped aff the bed.

At the funeral someone said,

> Wan thing Ah'll say fer the faither,
> he was jist made fer tha coffin. Pure statesman.
> In tha suit. Pinstriped. So dignified.

My mother says she's ready too.
She says,

> Ah've already been doon.
> Ah bought the plainest coffin Ah could find
> but when Ah got haime Ah thought it looked too Al Capone.
> So Ah went back an got oak.
> Eh was ever so nice.
> One thing Ah'll say fer they undertakers,
> they cannae dae enough fer yehs.

> Ach. Canada. It wiz a good move.

My mother tells me: Ach.

> In Canada, the faither died in his bed;
> the mither did the dishes
> an fell asleep.

Tom's on the phone.
He says when he went back and visited
St. Paul's, Shettleston Road, he asked,

> Whatever happened to Walter Bowdy?

And someone said,

> Walter Bowdy? Oh, he became an officer in the British Navy.
> One day his mind just opened up and he went away.

Tom sings into the telephone
in a Glasgow cowboy croon:

> *This heart ay mine – could never see*
> *What ev'rybod – y knew but me*
> *Just trustin yew – was mah great sin*
> *what can Ah dew – yew win a- gain.*

He can do twenty songs.

He can yodel *I Saw the Light.*
She holds out the phone.

Together, we listen.

(In the harmonica solo he always played with his eyes closed
face down, shoulders forward, feet going to the beat,
as if a strong wind was blowing him back
and he just couldn't help
tapping his toes.)

Arms.

A SHORT GLASWEGIAN GUIDE

Aboot: about

Ach: oh

Aff: off

Ah: I

Ahm: I'm

Aroond: around

Aw: all

Ay: of

Aye: closest translation = yes

Ayver: ever

Blether/Blaither: talk nonsense

Chanty-po: chamber pot

Clout: hit

Dae: do

Doon: down

Doot: doubt

Eh: he or oh

Ehm: him or well

Ehself/Ehsel: himself

Er: or

Faither: father

Fer: for

Fre: from

Gaunny: going to

Goan: going

Gie: give

Hae: have

Haime: home

Jist: just

Keek: look

Lalldy: trouble

Like the toot: fast

Loddy: men

Mah/meh/ma/me: my

Mither/maither: mother

Nae: not

Napper: head

Nayver: never

Noat: not

Oan: on

Of: ay

Oor: our

Oos: us

Oot: out

Peely wally: pale

Poot: put

Roond: round

Sehd: said

Teh/te/tae: to

Tha: that

Toon: town

Wan: one (thing)

Wain: child

Windae: window

Like winky: fast

Wallies: false teeth

Wis/Wiz/Wuz: was

Wi: with

Wull: will or well

Yeh/ye/yew/ yehs/yewz: you

Yehs'r: You are

Yer: your

Yersehl/yersel: yourself

Yin: one (person)

Annual Literary Competitions

(open to Canadians only)

Carter V. Cooper $15,000 Short Fiction Competition

$10,000 for the Best Story by an Emerging Writer

$5,000 for the Best Story by a Writer at Any Career Point

The 12 short-listed are published in the annual *CVC Short Fiction Anthology*
and the Canadian journal *ELQ/Exile: The Literary Quarterly*

Gwendolyn MacEwen $2,500 Poetry Competition

$2,000 for the Best Suite of Poetry

$500 for the Best Poem

Winners are published in *ELQ/Exile: The Literary Quarterly*

Details and Entry Forms at
www.TheExileWriters.com